PENGUIN BUSINESS
THE POWER OF IGNORED SKILLS

Manoj Tripathi is a sales and marketing professional. He is an avid reader, traveller and blogger. He writes on socio-economic issues and business solutions for leading business magazines.

THE POWER OF IGNORED SKILLS

Change the way
you think and decide

MANOJ TRIPATHI

PENGUIN
BUSINESS

An imprint of Penguin Random House

PENGUIN BUSINESS

Penguin Business is an imprint of the Penguin Random House group of companies
whose addresses can be found at global.penguinrandomhouse.com

Published by Penguin Random House India Pvt. Ltd
4th Floor, Capital Tower 1, MG Road,
Gurugram 122 002, Haryana, India

Penguin
Random House
India

First published in Penguin Business by Penguin Random House India 2024

Copyright © Manoj Tripathi 2020

All rights reserved

10 9 8 7 6 5 4 3 2 1

The views and opinions expressed in this book are the author's own and the facts are
as reported by him which have been verified to the extent possible, and the publishers
are not in any way liable for the same.

Please note that no part of this book may be used or reproduced in any manner for the
purpose of training artificial intelligence technologies or systems.

ISBN 9780143470397

Typeset in Adobe Garamond Pro
Printed at Replika Press Pvt. Ltd, India

This book is sold subject to the condition that it shall not, by way of trade
or otherwise, be lent, resold, hired out, or otherwise circulated without the
publisher's prior consent in any form of binding or cover other than that in
which it is published and without a similar condition including this condition
being imposed on the subsequent purchaser.

www.penguin.co.in

MIX
Paper | Supporting
responsible forestry
FSC™ C016779

To my dear mom and dad

CONTENTS

PREFACE

This book is all about the importance of skills, which are not so talked about but play a very significant role in our success.

Skills are the expertise or talent needed to do a task effectively. Simply put, you require skill to do anything and everything; currently, you are reading this book because of the skill of reading. You went to the market driving your car; thus, you exhibited a driving skill. In the market, while buying stuff, you compared two products; this means you displayed your evaluation and decision-making skill (good or bad). Therefore, skill is something that is very common and seems ordinary. Still, it plays an extraordinary role in our life as it determines our salary or earnings, respect and position in society.

Have you ever wondered why people who have an MBA education from Ivy League schools get paid more? These colleges are known to develop skills that are required to grow the business of the corporation.

Skills help us succeed in life. The best thing about a skill is that it can be acquired. That is why, immediately after an ordinary college degree, and despite not having many skills, people still get a job. It is because employers believe that if the attitude is right, the skill can be developed in their employees.

Through various anecdotes, I have tried to prove the importance of some necessary skills, which we generally tend to ignore. I am not trying to say that we don't believe in those skills, but having these skills is so common, that enough attention is not paid to them; hence, I have concluded that these are ignored skills.

To convince you about the importance of these skills, I have cited many examples from the ancient and contemporary world. Most of the cases are in the form of short stories to make things interesting. Of course, the purpose of this book is to share knowledge about life skills and social skills.

Now the question arises, despite knowing that skills are essential and that they help us in our lives, why do we ignore some of them? To arrive at the answer, let me ask you, isn't it true that our weakness is not visible to us? You know very well that you can become a better person by removing your weaknesses, but you still do not identify it yourself.

The same way, it's natural that something that is very obvious skips from our mind, or we keep procrastinating.

The nine ignored skills or concepts which are covered in this book are:

1. Power of Observation

2. Power of Connecting the Dots

3. Power of Communication

4. Power of Purpose

5. Power of Dreams

6. Power of Out-of-the-Box Thinking

7. Power of Perseverance

8. Power of Deep Diving

9. Power of Prediction

I am sure you have heard of each of these skills. Before reading any further, just ask yourself, have you actively tried to improve these skills? If yes, then I presume you are in the top or middle management of a company; if not, you are trying to jump into middle management.

While writing this book, I have chosen different kinds of skills to cover varied aspects; and therefore, created more opportunities for sharing various stories and examples. There are more than fifty short stories in this book, making things simple and interesting.

Enjoy reading!

CHAPTER 1

THE POWER OF OBSERVATION

"People's minds are changed through observation and not through argument."

– Will Rogers

Observation is an action or a process of carefully watching someone or something. Observation is simply a way of understanding the world we live in, but is it really simple to observe? What makes a few of us more observant and, on the contrary, why do others simply ignore or fail to register events around them?

Whenever someone from another organisation visits your company and presents their proposal or expertise, aren't you trying to observe their body language, dressing sense, communication, behaviour, confidence level, way of content delivery, and quality of content? All these observations help you form a perception about the visiting person and his organisation. Whether you observe actively or passively, your observation skills help you in your personal and professional life.

Our brain is always at work; it keeps observing things. You may never pay attention, but somehow subconsciously your brain registers events, analyses, and decides actions or reactions.

For instance, while driving, you pay attention to ensure that no one is crossing the road or coming in front of your car. Similarly, you automatically apply brakes while nearing a hairpin bend. This happens, because your brain observes, assesses and processes the information it is fed through your eyes or ears, and then takes the appropriate decision without you having to intervene.

Now, let's digress a bit from the present to the past, to understand how observation has helped humankind. Have you ever thought about why Homo sapiens (humans) are a superior species? Why are humans ruling the land despite being inferior to other animals in terms of physical strength, speed, and agility?

A child cannot survive for years without help from parents, whereas a three-month-old kitten can independently manage its life. A child takes almost a year to stand on its feet and walk, but a newborn calf manages to stand on its feet and starts floundering when it is just a few days old.

Imagine a fully-grown adult fighting with a two-year-old lion, who do you think is likely to win? The answer is obvious, but I'll leave it to you to decide.

Let us come back to the critical question, 'Why are Homo sapiens the superior species?'

The human race has evolved from a troglodyte to today's modern humans who are capable of making space stations.

The ability to think and transfer knowledge through generations has helped humans reach the pinnacle of success. In order to transfer knowledge, it's essential to gain knowledge first. Humans gain knowledge through observing the events around them or through someone else's experiences.

Thus, the key to human evolution is the ability to observe and think critically. Observation leads to knowledge. Then knowledge is transferred to fellow humans.

This transfer of learning became a possibility through communication. Long before the invention of scripts, how do you think information or learning passed through generations? It was through verbal communication. Ancient Indian religious and scientific learnings from Vedas were passed down generations via listening, *Sruti*, and memorising, *Smriti*, this tradition is still in practice in many folds of religious education.

Therefore, observation worked as a building block of knowledge.

If we study the ancient civilisations of Egypt, Central Asia, Latin America, Indus valley—we see that thousands of years ago, wise men researched medical science, astrology, and mathematics and wrote treatises with their observations. Generation after generation, people studied, documented, and improved the repository. All this happened because of observation-led learnings.

Malcolm Gladwell, in his brilliantly written book, *Blink*, has explained the importance of the phenomenon called 'thin-slicing'. He argues that the human brain can process a small amount of information, a thin slice, and draw incredible conclusions. This is made possible through a repository of data in our mind, which is accumulated through years of observation.

Today, we have powerful telescopes and satellites to help scientists calculate the precise date and time of the next eclipse or any other terrestrial phenomenon.

Have you ever wondered how thousands of years ago, Egyptians were able to forecast the next eclipse with precision?

Now, we have scientific evidence that many ancient civilisations knew about planetary movements, the solar system, and the position of stars. They did this without even having any advanced machinery back in those days.

Imagine the tedious task of noting the daily, weekly, monthly, and yearly variation in the position of planetary objects, and analysing them to predict the next planetary phenomenon accurately.

This extraordinary feat was possible because of years of minute observation.

Evidently, the knowledge we have today is an outcome of continuous learning, which was saved and passed on throughout human history. Thus, the power of observation and the ability to communicate has helped humans conquer the world.

In the next sections of this chapter, we will go through the evidence of the power of observation.

1.1 An Apple Can Change Everything

Three centuries ago, a man was enjoying the English summer under the shade of an apple tree. The apples were ripe and were falling here and there. The man observed the apples fall and wondered "why are the apples falling down?"

Falling of apple was not a unique phenomenon, but he reasoned with himself, "Why does an apple fall on the ground? Why downward, instead of falling sideways, or going straight into the sky?"

Indeed, the question was quite silly, but eventually, this man's observation of this inconsequential event led him to formulate the theory of gravity in the year 1667.

He went on to become a great scientist, Sir Isaac Newton.

Isn't it amazing that observation of even obvious things can be very radical, or open new doors that seem non-existent to most?

Let us take a coffee break, not in literal terms, but to understand how observation and actions can revolutionise how we all drink coffee today.

1.2 Coffee and Count of the Filter Cone

If we list the best gifts from the USA to the world, then in all possibility, it will be blue jeans, rock-n-roll, and coffee.

However, many do not know, coffee got a slow start in the US, and a revolt against the British King George III in 1773 led to the coffee revolution. The Boston Tea Party, as the revolt was called, was the reason behind the mass switch from tea to coffee in the US.

Fast forward 200 years, premium coffee shops, were gaining popularity in the United States in the early 1970s. To tap the growing market demand, an ambitious entrepreneur opened a new coffee shop in Seattle in 1971.

The new brand gained popularity among masses and was on the course to become what it is now. However, there was a twist in the story.

This coffee shop chain procured plastic cone filters from a company called Hammarplast.

One day, Howard Schultz, General Manager of Hammarplast, observed an interesting trend while inspecting through the sales records. He found that a small coffee shop chain in Seattle is buying an abnormally high number of plastic cone filters.

Interested and fascinated with this kind of sales, Howard decided to pay it a visit. During his visit to the coffee shop, he found nothing unusual; it was a typical coffee shop just like any other.

He asked for a coffee, and this is where he found the difference. Two things pleasantly surprised him: the employees' knowledge about coffee and second, their customer service.

He observed that none of the staff were rushing; they each talked calmly, discussed coffee tastes, and made suggestions to consumers based on their taste needs. Additionally, the ambience allowed customers to sit and sip while talking to friends and family.

Howard Schultz was so impressed, that he joined this coffee shop chain as the marketing director after some time. After a few years of working there, he had a difference of opinion with the owner and resigned. Somehow, he was so fascinated with the shop that he managed to acquire the chain later on.

Today, the turnover of this coffee chain is over 20 billion USD and has footprint worldwide. This coffee chain market capitalisation made Howard Schultz one of the wealthiest people in the world.

Any guesses?

Yes, you are right—it is Starbucks!

If there was a single most crucial thing, which Howard did right in his lifetime, it is that he observed.

He used the power of his observation to unfold the possibilities of future, unbox something extraordinary, and so did Newton in the earlier story.

Do you use the power of observation?

Yes, no, or maybe.

Your answer can be anything, but let me tell you that you are using the power of observation every day, without realising or thinking about it.

Previously in the chapter, I mentioned the connection between observation and humankind; let us explore it more.

1.3 Role of Observation in Human Life

The most common and straightforward method for getting information about everything around us is to observe. Hence, observation acts as a fundamental and primary way of getting information about anything.

However, it must be kept in mind that observation is not just seeing things, but it is all about carefully examining those things to make a sensible judgement about them.

Improving observation skills allows you to "listen" with more than just your ears, make better decisions, and form better perceptions. It also enhances the ability to interact with others and respond appropriately. These are both keys to success in professional and personal life. In the workplace, a good employee listens well and is aware of what is happening around him.

Observation is an integral part of learning. Theoretically, the most common form of learning is observational learning. Observational learning describes learning through watching others, retaining the information, and then replicating the observed behaviours.

There are several other learning theories, such as classical conditioning and operant conditioning. These theories help emphasise how direct experience, reinforcement, or punishment leads to learning in individuals.

However, one may argue that a great deal of learning happens indirectly; for example, imagine how a kid watches his parents waving at each other, and then imitates these actions. Kids learn through this process of watching and imitating others. In psychology, this is known as observational learning.

Observational learning continues throughout one's life, but it tends to be the most common during childhood, as children learn from elders and society. Observation also plays an essential role in the socialisation process. Children often learn how to behave, and respond to others by observing how their parents interact with each other and other people. That's why parents need to act a certain way, so children do not learn bad manners.

That's why, in popular culture, people judge parents based on their children's behaviour.

Famous Canadian–American psychologist, Albert Bandura, spent his life researching and learning through observation. Through experiments, he demonstrated that we are naturally inclined to engage in observational learning.

Children as young as 21 days old imitate facial expressions. Isn't it amazing?

In his famous Bobo doll experiment in 1961, Albert Bandura demonstrated that young children would imitate an adult model's violent actions. In the experiment, children were shown a film, in which an adult repeatedly hit a giant, inflatable balloon doll. After viewing the film clip, children were allowed to play with a real Bobo doll, just like the one they saw in the film.

The research proved, that the children who had seen violent behaviour in the film clip were violent with Bobo doll; as opposed to other kids, who had not seen the film clip. This proves the point that children's behaviour largely depends on the culture surrounding them. This experiment raises the question of the impact of violent movies, television programmes, and video games on children.

Psychologists Craig Anderson and Karen Dill established the link between video game violence and aggressive behaviour. Through the experiment, they proved students who played a violent video game behaved more aggressively than those who had not played violent games.

Later on, the American Psychological Association concluded that exposure to violent interactive video games increased aggressive thoughts, feelings, and behaviours.

All these researches prove the fact that observational learning is prevalent in children.

We Indians are fond of cricket; hence, let me take you through the example of cricket.

1.4 You Will Enjoy More If You Are Observant

It was 16 March 2012, Sachin Tendulkar was batting, and Dale Steyn was bowling. It was the third ball of the seventh over, Dale Steyn bowled and Sachin Tendulkar played beautiful cover drive. The whole stadium erupted with joy; those who were watching the match on TV sets also started clapping. Millions watched the shot and enjoyed it.

Only a few people observed the entire proceeding. For them, Dale Steyn bowled over pitch in-swing ball, just outside the off-stump, Sachin Tendulkar read the ball before the ball landed on the pitch, extended his left foot, reached the ball, and hit it with great timing; keeping the face of the bat closed, so that shot remain grounded, and piercing the fielder standing at mid-off and covers. Sachin's toe was in the direction of the shot, which he played.

The next day, those who had observed *how* Sachin played the cover drive shot were able to perform a similar cover drive (they were able to imitate it because they had learnt from observation). Whereas, those who only watched Sachin's shot, blamed the pitch they were playing on for not being able to replicate the cover drive themselves.

Thus, those who observed closely learnt much more than others who just watched.

Observation helps us learn faster and better. It is a painful and time-consuming process, but is a sure shot recipe of winning. You will enjoy this more if you know the proceedings well; observation is the best way to understand them.

Now the question arises, why are some of us more observant than others? It largely depends on the natural flair of curiosity. Let us understand this in detail.

1.5 How Does Curiosity and Observation Help in the Decision-Making Process?

Curiosity means a strong desire to know or learn about something. Observation emerging from curiosity is the first and essential step in the decision-making process.

A curious person does not accept anything easily. He always has scepticism towards everything he sees and hears. Curious people always ask questions, i.e., they try to challenge the status quo and search for new answers.

Being curious can help you know more and make better decisions. This can give you an edge over others.

When you are curious, you can distinguish between the situations in which decisions need to be made on the spot or in the future. Curiosity generally stimulates other processes, that help you in decision-making like questioning, comparing, inquiring about things, experimentation, visualisation, scepticism, categorisation, identification of different patterns, imaginative thought, evaluation, logical reasoning, prediction, inference, etc. All these processes will lead you towards suitable decisions.

Observation allows you to notice important things to gather information. No doubt, if you are observant, then you can become a good decision-maker.

With curious observation, you can make your decision-making process easy and effective. When taking a decision, think about the problem repeatedly. Think and visualise the whole scenario in your mind to predict the outcome of your decision.

Curiosity during the decision-making process leads to dissatisfaction i.e., you do not feel content with the decision, and consequently, dissatisfaction leads to improvement in decision-making abilities. Therefore, the more curious we are, the more we will observe, and thus, our decision-making ability would be better.

Good observation skill helps in overcoming statistical bias. Let's understand this through an example from mythology.

1.6 Observation Is Above Statistics

As per Hindu mythology, Narad Muni is one of the most prominent devotees of Lord Vishnu. He used to chant "Nayaran Narayan", the other name of Lord Vishnu, with every breath.

One day, he went to Lord Vishnu and asked, "My Lord, who is your biggest devotee?" Narad Muni was quite sure that Lord Vishnu would take his name. Lord Vishnu said, "My biggest devotee is a poor farmer on Earth." Narad Muni was quite surprised and disturbed. He immediately decided to go and see this farmer. He had divine power, which he used to become invisible. When he got near that farmer, he noticed that the farmer chanted "Nayaran Narayan" only twice in 24 hours. The farmer was occupied in agriculture, feeding cows and buffalos, gathering wood for cooking food, etc.

Narad Muni went back to Lord Vishnu and said, "My Lord, there seems to be an error in your judgement, the farmer chanted 'Nayaran Narayan' only twice, while I chant almost 1,000 times in a day; therefore, statistically, I should be the winner, so please let me know, how this farmer can be your biggest devotee?" Lord Vishnu smiled and told him that all the queries would be answered, but he has to do a critical task for him before that. Narad Muni said, "My Lord, I am always in your duty; please let me know what I need to do?"

Lord Vishnu gave Narad Muni a small *diya* (lamp), which was lit. Lord Vishnu said, "O dear, you have to go around the Earth, and come back within 24 hours, just keep in mind that the diya must not get off." Narad Muni had the divine power of flying; hence, he was very confident that he would successfully perform the task. As soon as he left the place with the diya, he realised that it's not so easy to keep it lit, as the wind was a threat to blowing it off. He somehow, covered the diya, and suddenly a storm came, Narad Muni had an uphill task to keep the lamp lit, and somehow, he crossed that area. He was feeling tired and thirsty, but he was worried that if he stops, he might not reach Lord Vishnu within 24 hours; hence, he continued to fly. Next, there was heavy rain. Again, he was in deep problem; with a lot of effort, he managed to cross that area also. Finally, with great effort and pain, he reached to Lord Vishnu's abode and claimed that he managed to complete the task successfully, within 24 hours. Lord Vishnu said, "Indeed, you have completed the task within 24 hours, and ensured that diya is lit, so no doubt you are successful in your task; but now tell me how many times you have chanted 'Nayaran Narayan' in the last 24 hours?" Narad Muni realised that he had not chanted "Nayaran Narayan" even a single time in that period. Narad Muni said, "O Lord, I was so busy performing the task that I missed chanting your name."

Lord Vishnu said, "Dear Narad, the poor farmer is also performing tasks which are equally difficult, yet he manages to chant my name twice a day, now tell me, isn't he is my biggest devotee?" Narad Muni humbly accepted this fact.

The moral of the story is, if you go by pure statistics, you can commit mistakes. You have to observe all the facts around the statistics to reach a correct conclusion.

Does observation help in our studies? Let's understand it from the story below.

1.7 Observation and Study

Louis Agassiz, the famous Swiss biologist and professor, at Harvard, had a unique way of teaching. He was master of in-depth comparison and held a distinguished position in the studies of life science and zoological education.

Once, he placed a fish specimen on the table in front of one of his postgraduate students and asked him to find out more about the fish, without causing any harm. Louis Agassiz then left the class for some other reason.

The student watched the fish for some time and casually wrote for almost an hour until he felt confident that he knew all there was to know about that fish.

But his professor did not turn up that day, and similarly, the professor didn't come for the next few days. The student grew frustrated at first, but eventually, he understood Agassiz's plan: the professor wanted him to observe the fish more deeply.

After a few days of study, he finally began to notice finer details that had escaped his vision previously—how the scales of the fish were shaped and the patterns they made; how the colour of fish differed in different parts; the placement of the teeth, the shape of each tooth and so on. When his professor finally returned, and the student explained all that he had learnt. Agassiz replied, "I am not happy with the findings," and walked out of the room.

The student was disappointed that the professor had discarded all his efforts, but he gathered the courage to try again. He sidelined all his previous notes to start afresh. He studied the fish for several hours a day for an entire week. When he met with the professor next the student had produced a work that was a milestone in studying that species of fish.

After his investigation of the sunfish, the student wrote, "I had learnt the art of comparing objects based on a naturalist's work."

Professor Agassiz is fondly remembered as the best professor after Greek philosopher Socrates, and his legacy continued with many of his students becoming famous professors and distinguished scholars.

Do you know, observation has enabled many discoveries? Let's find out.

1.8 Role of Observation in Scientific Discovery

"To acquire knowledge, one must study;

But to acquire wisdom, one must observe."

– Marilyn vos Savant

Invariably every scientific investigation begins with an observation.

In his famous book, *A Brief History of Time*, Stephen Hawking noted, *"good scientific theories must be built on a large class of observations."*

Observations are the basis of scientific theories.

Creativity usually begins by observing the situation and paying close attention to how problems and challenges are being solved. In the case of product innovation, existing systems, products, or natural occurrences can be applied to a new challenge.

1.9 How Did Edward Jenner Invent the Smallpox Vaccine?

In the middle of the eighteenth century, smallpox was a deadly disease for humans. It killed about one-third of those infected. Survivors often bore scars on their faces and other parts of the body. It was a leading cause of blindness back then. Thus, it was a big challenge for physicians and scientists to find the solution to this deadly disease.

The British physician Edward Jenner was born in 1749. Jenner proved that infection with cowpox could protect a person from smallpox infection. Cowpox was a cattle disease which could also infect humans, but it was not so deadly and harmful.

While Jenner was talking to his milkmaid, she claimed that she would never get smallpox because she had had cowpox. Similarly, he observed that many other dairy workers also believed that cowpox infection protected them from smallpox.

Jenner was astonished to learn this, and he decided to investigate this belief. Thus, he decided to experiment on his gardener's son. He scratched a cowpox sore on a milkmaid's hand, then rubbed his hand on the arm of the eight-year-old boy, Phipps. The boy got ill, but was fine after a few days, i.e. he had recovered from cowpox.

After a few weeks, Jenner tried to infect Phipps with smallpox using the same method with a fresh smallpox sore. Phipps, however, did not contract smallpox. Jenner replicated the experiment with other people and published his findings in a leading journal.

Jenner was successful in creating a vaccine against smallpox, which helped eradicate this disease from the world. Thanks to the global mass vaccination programme, the World Health Organisation eventually declared smallpox eradicated from the planet in 1980.

1.10 Benjamin Franklin and His Observations

In the mid-eighteenth century, most people believed that wet clothing and dampness in the air caused the common cold. However, Benjamin Franklin observed that sailors, who were continually wearing wet clothing, were not always suffering from cold; thus, something was wrong in people's belief about the common cold.

After some analysis, he eventually concluded that people often caught a cold from one another, when they sat close by and breathed the same air. Before widespread research on viruses and germs, Franklin had figured out that common cold transmitted through the air.

Therefore, by observing sailors, he convinced the world that something that was transmitted between people caused common cold. It was a big revelation, and this led to microbiology research and the invention of medicines for cold.

Benjamin's Role in Electricity

People had started using electricity in the mid-eighteenth century, but not to the extent we do today. Back then, people used electricity for magic tricks, by creating sparks and shocks to amaze people. Scientists were experimenting for centuries, but could not get much success in the application of electricity. Hence, there was no practical use of electricity.

Benjamin Franklin, a curious and inventive thinker, studied electricity in detail and came up with a hypothesis.

Franklin observed several similarities between electricity and lightning as they both created light, made a loud noise when they exploded, were attracted to metal, had a particular smell, etc. Thus, Franklin got the idea that electricity and lightning were the same thing. Franklin wrote his thoughts on electricity in several letters to his scientist friends who lived in London. The scientists found Franklin's observation very interesting, so in 1751, they published them in a book titled, *Experiments and Observations on Electricity.*

Franklin decided to prove his hypothesis. He desperately needed an object to get close enough to the clouds to attract lightning.

His plan required something tall, like a hill or a tall building; but in Philadelphia, USA, they had neither a mountain nor a tall building.

He came up with an idea which involved a key and a kite.

Instead of getting himself close to the lightning, he attached a metal key to a kite and flew it up, to attract the lightning, and it worked.

Franklin proved with this experiment that lightning and electricity were the same thing.

However, even after successfully proving his hypothesis about electricity, he didn't stop. He firmly believed that the knowledge about electricity must be used for practical purposes that should help humankind. Still, the larger question was – what could the practical use of this new finding be?

Fire caused by lightning was common in tall buildings in those days. Franklin decided to do something about it. Franklin knew that lightning usually hit the highest part of a building, and the electrical current in lightning could start a fire. Therefore, he invented the lightning rod. It was made of metal and attached to the highest point on a building. Lightning hit the rod instead of the building, and the electrical current from the lightning went into the ground without damaging it.

Do you know this invention has saved thousands of lives?

Thus, with the help of his observational skill, Benjamin Franklin contributed to humanity's progress.

1.11 Velcro's Jungle Connection

One day, Georges de Mestral, a Swiss engineer, was trekking in the jungle along with his dog. He observed that burdock burrs (a kind of seed), were stuck to his clothing and even his dog's fur. He tried to remove them, but it was not so easy. He examined the burrs through a microscope and realised that it was the hook-like structure that tangled with cloth or fur. He wondered whether the burrs could be made into something useful. He was so convinced with his idea of creating synthetic burrs, that he continued his efforts for more than a decade, and finally, he found success. He called his invention *Velcro* and patented it in 1955. We use Velcro in our bags, shoes, etc.

I hope you agree that this is a perfect example of curious observation.

If you do not know what Velcro is, please refer to the picture below:

1.12 Alexander Fleming and His Anti-Bacterial Medicine

Tuberculosis and Pneumonia are bacterial diseases. Both of these deadly diseases killed millions of humans, and there was no treatment for either in the early twentieth century.

Many scientists were working on finding a cure for these bacterial diseases. Alexander Fleming was one of them, but he was in the middle of an experiment when he had to leave for some urgent work. After many days of absence from his lab, when he returned, he found it messy and began to clean some of the glass plates on which he had been growing a certain kind of bacteria. While cleaning, suddenly, he observed an odd thing: one of the plates had been contaminated by mould. Surprisingly, the area around the mould looked free of bacteria. Fleming's observation indicated that a causal relationship might exist between mould or something produced by the mould, which might prevent bacterial growth. This rather small observation of Fleming's led to a series of scientific tests that resulted in new knowledge, and finally, Penicillin was invented to treat bacterial infections. Penicillin helped cure the deadly pneumonia; thus, millions of lives have been saved.

I hope you agree, that if creativity can be sparked by observing the environment and the situations we experience daily, the possibilities are infinite. Creativity can come at any moment, in virtually any form. Having an open mind can lead to unbelievable outcomes. In companies, the marketers, product developers, salespeople, and CEOs often observe and think about how observation can relate to their product or service. Allow yourself to dream, imagine, and create. Organisations, which are dedicated to challenging the status quo, and continuously seeking creative solutions, are often the winners in today's fast-paced market.

Now the question arises, why have I termed observation as an ignored skill? You might have noticed the importance of observation while going through the various anecdotes mentioned in this chapter. Tell me honestly, how many times have you tried to develop this skill?

There is not much discussion on this topic, hardly any educational courses are offered on it, and not many books have been written on observation skills. The simple reason behind this very common: it is usually ignored.

Now I hope you will try your best to develop observation skills through concentration and curiosity.

The next chapter is about your ability to connect various independent events to understand their implications.

———•———

CHAPTER 2

THE POWER OF CONNECTING THE DOTS

"You can't connect the dots looking forward; you can only connect them looking backwards."

– Steve Jobs

Connecting the dots means putting various facts and ideas together to see a complete picture. It can help us understand the historical perspective in the true sense and reveal why things are happening.

Our ability to connect dots offers great insights. The knowledge we possess is the most significant enabler in developing this skill of connecting the dots. Things are related to each other; our action and thought process result from prior experience and will be based on future consequences. The incidental results of various past factors will impact future events. Therefore, the skill of connecting the dots helps us plan our activities better.

If you develop this skill, it will help you make informed decisions which will have long-term implications.

In this chapter, I will try to help you understand the beauty of connecting the dots through various examples.

2.1 Bombay Dreams and Its Suez Connection

Mumbai, or Bombay, wasn't always this vibrant and developed despite being a business hub in India.

If you look at Bombay's story, you will see so many dots, and when you connect them, you get the story behind the Bombay's success.

In 1534, the Ruler of Gujarat, Bahadur Shah, ceded Mumbai to the Portuguese. At that point of time, Mumbai was nothing but sleeping coastal village of seven islands. For the next 127 years, Mumbai was under Portuguese rule, until 1661, when Prince Charles II of England married the Portuguese princess Catherine of Braganza.

Prince Charles II received Mumbai as a gift, a small port town with a population of little over 10,000 people.

At the same time, competition in trade was rising with the arrival of British East India Company, which established its first major trading hub in Surat in 1612.

This era also saw the conflict between the resurgent Maratha power and the Mughals. Due to continuous skirmishes between these two forces, East India Company was desperately looking for an alternate trading hub and headquarters.

Seizing the opportunity in 1668, British East India Company took Bombay from the Crown and developed it as their trading hub. This was the start of Bombay's story.

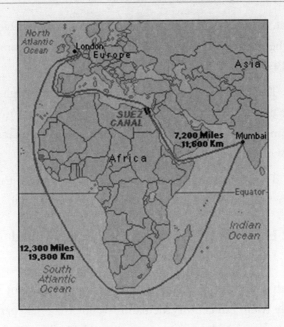

By 1675, the population of Mumbai had grown to 60,000 people and the port city was witnessing ever-increasing growth in business and prosperity, but one event was yet to happen which would change the course of Bombay's history—the opening of Suez Canal.

Suez Canal, a narrow passage connecting the Mediterranean Sea to the Red Sea, opened on November 17, 1869. This small canal, little less than 200 km long, changed the fate of Bombay.

Due to this canal, the distance between London and Mumbai was reduced by about 40 per cent. Cargo ships began to pass through the Arabian Sea while going to the eastern part of Asia; this made Bombay a significant port. Soon Bombay's sea trading business soared. Due to higher cotton export, cotton mills started mushrooming in Bombay.

They say success brings success, and it was right in the case of Mumbai. Being an export hub also made Mumbai a financial hub, and it emerged as the financial capital of India.

Thus, in Mumbai's story, a few dots connect to its transfer to the British Crown and to the Suez Canal.

2.2 How the US Government's Policy Killed Indian Cotton Farmers

With Mumbai becoming the hub of cotton mills, by the early twentieth century, demand for raw material soared. Farmers in Maharashtra, Gujarat, and Madhya Pradesh grabbed the opportunity. Cotton became the 'cash crop', giving profitable earning to farmers.

Fast forward to the twenty-first century, globalisation makes one wonder how a decision taken thousands of kilometres away affects someone sitting in a remote village in India.

To grow cotton, most of the farmers depend on credit for their financial needs. The repayment of loans depends on the yield of the crop, and for over a century, the supply-demand gap had ensured the balance remained skewed towards Indian cotton farmers.

By the 1960s, India's cotton supremacy was challenged and overtaken by the US, as it became the largest cotton producer. With China at the second position and India at the distant third, the US was not happy with the continuous challenge it faced in business.

US farmers informed their government officials that exporting cotton at a lesser price than India and China was challenging and hence, they feared they won't be able to export cotton.

To defeat China and India on the pricing turf, the US government announced heavily subsidised cultivation and cotton exports for its farmers. This action flooded the market with cheaper cotton from the US, and cotton prices dropped across the world, damaging the Indian and Chinese cotton industry's earnings.

In India, this resulted in a slowdown in the cotton industry, which forced factories to shut operations in Mumbai, Surat, and other parts of the country. Thousands lost their jobs, and inadvertently, millions suffered in the hinterlands of the country.

The prospect of uncertain, low-income futures led to many suicides and a max exodus of farmers to towns in search of menial jobs.

Thus, a decision made 12,000 km away from India led to the suicide of thousands of Indian cotton farmers.

However, since 2019, India has become the largest cotton producer once again, with China trailing in the second position. However, the cotton market is still uncertain, and now, instead of the US government, the market is mainly dependent on private players in the agricultural industry.

We are on the subject of farming, so let me share another incident related to farming in India.

2.3 The Green Revolution in India and Its Connection to the Vietnam War

India gained independence in 1947. The British had drained India, leaving its economy in tatters, industries in shambles, and the populace at the heaven's mercy.

The food production in India was not enough to feed its population of 360 million. On the contrary, the United States was producing much more wheat, than its consumption. US enacted a law, PL480, under which the US was giving free wheat to countries in distress. Obviously, it was part of their diplomacy, but it was still a noble gesture.

Upon request from the Indian government, the US agreed to give them free wheat. This programme was called "ship to mouth".

As India was getting free wheat, there was lethargy amongst Indian politicians as well as bureaucracy. No real efforts were made to increase food grain production in India. However, things changed when the US went to war with Vietnam.

India morally supported Vietnam in the war, which irked the US President, Lyndon B. Johnson. He decided to reduce the supply of wheat to India, to teach them a lesson.

India's situation became so grim, that the then Indian prime minister, Mr. Lal Bahadur Shastri, had to request the citizens to fast one day every week. After a lot of persuasions, the US resumed supply of wheat to India. This episode was enough for the Indian government to open their eyes, and focus on increasing farm productivity.

The Indian government deputed the best agricultural scientists to work out a solution, and help was sought from Mexico, which had seen an agricultural revolution.

With continuous focus of this subject, within five years, by 1971, India achieved self-reliance in food grain production, and the import of US wheat under PL480 was no longer needed.

Today, India stands tall in the global food supply chain, and features as a top grower of agricultural products in the reports of FAO (Food and Agriculture Organisation of the United Nations).

2.4 Canada's Connection to Uttar Pradesh and Bihar

You might be wondering as to what do people of UP and Bihar have to do with Canada and, similarly, what do people of north-east India have to do with the Middle East. Yes, you are right. Actively, there is no correlation between them, but passively there is.

Let me explain.

In the mid-1950s, many Punjabis migrated to Canada, thus leaving behind a workforce vacuum due to the shortage of agricultural labourers. Therefore, labourers from Uttar Pradesh and Bihar migrated to Punjab searching for greener pastures. In those days, labourers' conditions used to be very bad in Uttar Pradesh and Bihar; migration to Punjab helped them live a better life, and these migrant labourers started sending money back to their villages.

Thus, indirectly, Punjabis living the Canadian dream created an opportunity for people of Uttar Pradesh and Bihar.

In the same manner, once the oil economy boomed in the Middle East, people from Kerala moved there for construction and other labour-intensive jobs. This movement left Kerala with a workforce shortage. North-east Indians filled the gap in Kerala's workforce as there weren't many job opportunities in their homeland. Thus, the economic boom in the Middle East indirectly helped the people of north-east India.

The purpose of this example is to tell you that the implication of any event is widespread; our actions could affect many people, even the ones who are not on our radar.

The government and its policies play a significant role in our life. Let's go through an example in which, I have tried to highlight the government's policy mistakes.

2.5 How Government Policies Can Affect State Economies

Industries need raw material to manufacture goods. Heavy industries are the ones that act as enablers for small enterprises. Iron and steel industries are an example of heavy industries as their finished products are used in small industries to make household things. Thus, heavy industries are popularly called mother industries.

Most of the heavy industries need minerals. India is a mineral-rich country, however, deposits are confined to the states of Orissa, Jharkhand, Bihar, Madhya Pradesh, etc. In an ideal world, states with rich deposits should get the benefit of their mineral-rich soil.

When India got independence, there was a demand that there should be equal opportunity to all the states to produce goods. In principle, it was a good idea as it looked like it provided an equal opportunity for all.

Freight Equalisation Policy, 1952, was adopted by the Government of India to facilitate the balanced growth of the industry across the country. This meant a factory could be set up anywhere in India, and the Central government would subsidise the transportation of minerals.

Ideally, the industries would benefit if they set up a manufacturing unit near the source of raw material, as it would have reduced logistical costs. However, due to the Freight Equalisation Policy, the transportation cost was taken out of the equation, resulting in industrialists putting up factories in Gujarat, Maharashtra, and Tamil Nadu.

These states had an added advantage over mineral-rich states in the form of the coast, which was used for export and import. Thus, the government took away the advantage from mineral-rich states in the name of equal opportunity. This defective policy remained in force until 1993 when the government scrapped it, but it drained every possibility of bringing prosperity to the nation's mineral-rich areas.

After-effects of this policy can still be seen in the poor and undeveloped states of Jharkhand, Orissa, and Madhya Pradesh.

Sometimes, a solution that seems to be working, becomes part of the problem. Let me share a story.

2.6 The Snake Effect

The snake effect occurs when an attempted solution to a problem makes the problem worse. This term originated as an anecdote.

The story goes back to an incident in British India. Unfortunately, there were too many venomous cobra snakes in Delhi then. People were dying due to snakebites, and it became scary for everyone to step out of their houses. The governor had to get into action to stop this menace and offered money for every dead snake. He thought, once all snakes are killed, the problem would be solved.

The results of the reward programme were great; a large number of snakes were killed for the reward. The governor thought that his idea has worked.

Eventually, however, it led to some unwanted consequences. After a short-term dip in the snake population, surprisingly, the numbers started going up again.

This happened because a few people began breeding snakes for income. When this news reached the governor, the reward programme was discontinued, resulting in the snake breeders setting the now-worthless snakes free. As a result, the snake population increased further. The simple solution to a problem made the situation even worse.

A similar incident occurred in Vietnam, which was a French colony earlier. The administration realised that there were too many rats in Hanoi, and the spread of plague was imminent. Therefore, they created a reward programme that paid a prize for each rat killed. To obtain the reward, people needed to provide a severed rat tail. As expected, after the initial success of the programme, people started noticing rats with no tails. This happened because the rat catchers would capture rats, cut off their tails, and then release them back into the sewers to breed and produce more rats, thereby increasing their profits. Obviously, the reward programme was called off.

The unintended consequence of a well-intentioned idea sometimes makes the problem worse.

Let me share another example of an idea going wrong.

2.7 How a Logical Decision Proved to Be Wrong

During 1957–58, millions of Chinese people died because of hunger. The food grain production was inadequate for a population of 635 million.

Back then, the Chinese believed that birds and rodents eat some food grain; hence, if these birds and rodents were killed, it will lead to additional food grain for people. Therefore, the then president of China, Mao Tse Tung, commanded Chinese people all over the country to come out of their houses to bang pots or utensils and make the sparrows fly continuously, with the idea that they would die out of exhaustion, which, in March of 1958, people did.

Sparrows also were caught in nets, poisoned, and killed. There was a widespread belief that shooting birds would bring prosperity and, by some estimates, a billion birds died.

However, ecology does not work this way.

When the sparrows were killed, crop production and food grain availability indeed increased, but with time, something else happened, which was completely unexpected. Pests of rice and other crop multiplied to a magnitude never seen before, and as a result, crops failed. There was deficient food grain production. Starvation due to shortage of food grain led to the death of an estimated 35 million Chinese people.

Chinese ornithologists (those who study birds), had found that, while adult tree sparrows mostly eat food grains and fruits, their babies, like those of common house sparrows tend to eat insects. By killing the sparrows, Mao and the Chinese people, had saved the crops from sparrows, but as a result, insects got a free run in the absence of any predator.

Finally, 1960, Mao ordered sparrows to be conserved. This proves the fact that we value something only in its absence.

The beauty of ecology lies in the fact that everything plays a role in our life.

During school days, you might have come across a dilemma about how mathematics helps you in real life—algebra, geometry, trigonometry, calculus, statistic, permutation and combination gave nightmares to many.

Let me share an exciting story involving war and a mathematician.

2.8 How a Mathematician Helped Allied Forces Win World War II

During World War II, Germany had an edge because of its naval strength. German U-boats unleashed terror throughout Europe, but US shores were also well within the German submarine's attack range. Do you know, during the first three months of 1942, German U-boats sank more than 100 ships off North America's east coast, in the Gulf of Mexico and the Caribbean Sea? Many of those ships were within sight of land.

In war, communication plays a very important role in the armed forces. German forces were using the Enigma machine to send wireless communication internally. The Enigma machine was developed in Germany shortly after World War I, and was used to encode and decode messages. For the next two decades, the German military refined the technology until it became their primary means of secret communication during World War II. Enigma technology continuously altered throughout the war, making the challenge of breaking German cyphers extremely difficult.

British forces wanted to break the code to know the internal communication of German troops. The British army gave this responsibility to Alan Turing, a mathematician. He made a range of code-breaking machines for cracking German cyphers, which included an electromagnetic device, called the Bombe, which countered the German Enigma machine.

Though it's not possible to quantify the exact impact of Turing's contributions through breaking the code, some military historians estimate that the war would have been continued for at least another couple of years and two million more lives would have been lost if Alan Turing and his team hadn't cracked the way to decode German communication.

Without Turing and his team members' efforts, the allies would have continued to face a severe disadvantage against the German forces.

Shortly after World War II, Alan Turing was awarded the Order of the British Empire for his work.

Do you know Alan Turing is known as the father of the computer, and also the father of today's artificial intelligence?

Alan Turing is considered to be the father of modern computer science. He formed the concept of the algorithms and computations with one of his inventions called the Turing machine.

Turing moved to London in the mid-1940s, and began working for the National Physical Laboratory. Turing was instrumental in designing the Automatic Computing Engine, and ultimately created a ground-breaking blueprint for store-programme computers. Later on, his concept was used as a model by tech corporations worldwide for several years, influencing the English Electric DEUCE design and the American Bendix G-15—credited by many in the technology industry as the world's first personal computer.

Nowadays, artificial intelligence is a buzzword, but do you know that Turing played an important role in bringing artificial intelligence to our lives? Turing wrote a paper in a journal in 1950, with the title, "Computing machinery and intelligence", and proposed an experiment known as the "Turing Test" with an effort to create an intelligence design standard for the technology industry. In the last several decades, the test has significantly contributed to the field of artificial intelligence.

By the way, the British armed forces have also played a role in your life. Don't you know? OK, let me help you with another anecdote.

2.9 Cell Phones and British Armed Forces

It will not be wrong to say that mobile phones have become an integral part of our lives. Research shows that we spend more than four hours every day using a mobile phone.

In the late 1960s, the British Ministry of Defence decided it wanted flat-screens to replace bulky and expensive cathode ray tubes (like the black and white television sets of the old days), in its military vehicles. Scientists suggested liquid crystal displays (LCDs), but the problem was that they only really worked at high temperatures. So, they knew that this solution was not feasible. British Ministry of Defence requested George Gray at the University of Hull to work out ways to make LCDs function at room temperature. After a lot of effort, he succeeded by inventing a molecule known as 5CB. This molecule helped LCDs work at room temperature. By the late-1970s and early-1980s, almost 90 per cent of the world's LCD devices contained 5CB. Later on, the same technology was replicated in cell phone screens. This molecule is still in use in some cheap watches and calculators. Thus, George Grey has contributed to our most used device i.e., the smartphone.

Therefore, there is a story behind every success. If we know the genesis of success, it is easier to learn and use that learning in real life. It's not easy to connect the dots, because it is impossible to understand the story or simply enjoy it without knowing the facts and the complete background. This skill can help you to get an edge over others and excel in life.

So, what is required to develop this skill?

The answer is again curiosity, more comprehensive knowledge, and a little bit of common sense.

In the next chapter, we will go through the importance of communication. Just keep in mind that no communication is also a form of communication. Confused? Do not worry; let me make it easy.

If your partner is not talking to you, or not picking your call, aren't they communicating something?

CHAPTER 3

THE POWER OF COMMUNICATION

"A man's character may be learned from the adjectives which he habitually uses in conversation."

– Mark Twain

Communication is fundamental for the existence and survival of humans. It is a process of creating and sharing ideas, information, facts, views, feelings, etc. with people to reach a common understanding.

Leaders have used communication to motivate and align people.

There are broadly two types of communication; verbal and non-verbal. Verbal communication is the use of words to share information with other people. It can include both spoken and written communication. At the same time, non-verbal signals, are word-less communication like body postures, facial expressions, hand movements, gestures, eye contact, attitude, and tone of the voice.

According to you, which type of communication do we use more, verbal or non-verbal? If your answer is verbal, I am sorry, you are wrong.

According to research on interpersonal communication, 93 per cent of communication is non-verbal.

Another study shows that the reason for 90 per cent of fights was not what someone said, but due to the tone something was said in. This shows the importance of communication. Indeed, words are powerful, but the tone in which the words are spoken is often more powerful. Sometimes, not-so-soothing words said in a cheerful or light tone have a different impact on the person, while the most pleasant words remain ineffective. The power of tone is, no doubt, a key factor behind the success of an individual. Words are often used as a mode of communication, but the real weapon is the tone, which can cement or end a relationship. You know the pen is mightier than the sword; similarly, it may be said that tone is mightier than words.

Your use of non-verbal signals will help you make friends, connect with others well, express what's on your mind, and build better relationships at home and office.

In an earlier chapter, I asked, "Imagine a grown adult, lest a child, to fight with a two-year-old lion, who do you think is more likely to win?" The answer is the two-year-old lion. This is enough to prove how difficult it would have been for humans to survive among animals almost 2.5 million years ago.

If humans are so weak in comparison to animals, then how have they survived and thrived?

Some pundits would answer that the ability to light a fire has given humans an edge over other animals. Indeed, that would have helped immensely, but there is something more important which helped humans. We are the only species that can transfer knowledge between generations. That is why, every generation is wiser than the previous generation, and as a result, humans have been accumulating knowledge.

Learning is the most important thing. Animals learn through trial and error, but humans largely learn from others' experiences. We know about neutrons and protons, gravity on the moon, chemical composition of water, treatment of diseases, power and torque of your car, etc. I hope you will agree with me that neither of these things were invented nor discovered by you. It was someone else who did all experiments, which we learnt and acquired the knowledge from.

Initially, homo sapiens might have used only body language to communicate, then the verbal method might have emerged, and after that, some written signal would have preceded alphabets. Therefore, initially, it was mostly face-to-face communication, but later on, with a book's help, face-to-face communication was no longer required, and now with the internet, communication and knowledge transfer has reached a new height.

Therefore, the ability to transmit knowledge has helped humans conquer the world.

Even today, those who are learned are respected more, because their ability to contribute to society is more. A historical perspective tells us that communication has been critical in humans' success.

After many years of research, the Carnegie Institute of Technology concluded, *"85 percent of your financial success is due to your personality and ability to communicate, negotiate, and lead. Shockingly, only 15 percent, due to the technical knowledge you have."*

Indra Nooyi, ex-chairman and CEO of PepsiCo, says, "You can't over-invest in communication."

You will be surprised to know that British Prime Minister Mrs. Margret Thatcher hired a National Theatre tutor, to improve her communication.

Are you using communication skills effectively? If not, please work on it. What is most important in communication is your content, tone, and body language.

Steve Jobs is known as one of the most prominent innovators as well as communicators. In the year 2001, MP3 players were famous. Steve Jobs had to announce the launch of a new iPod, i.e., the competitor of an MP3 player. During the pre-launch rehearsal, Steve Job's technical team informed that Apple's just 1.8-inch device has 5 GB data, and that's the biggest USP of product. Steve Jobs thought from the customer's angle and declared in the launch event, that he is proud to launch the iPod, which means 1,000 songs in the customer's pockets. You will agree that for customers, the 1,000 song narrative is more attractive than the 5 GB data narrative. Therefore, Steve Jobs made an impact on the new product through his customer-centric communication.

Effective communication has the ability to solve complex problems. Let's find out how the British prime minister, Winston Churchill, used his communication skill to persuade his fellow citizens to fight against Germans.

3.1 How Winston Churchill Changed the Course of World War II with the Help of His Speech

World War II started on September 1, 1939. With the help of Italy, Germany defeated France on July 24, 1940.

Germany had defeated France, Belgium, and the Netherlands. Their next target was Britain. There was widespread fear in Britain about the war.

Lord Halifax, the foreign secretary of Britain, had a difference of opinion with Churchill, and he requested him to negotiate peace terms with Hitler. Lord Halifax informed him that Italy was ready to become a mediator. Churchill was not at all in favour of bowing down against Hitler. He was determined to fight with German forces, but for that, he had to convince the British parliament, which was an uphill task. The British parliament was in favour of the referendum of citizens (to decide about fighting Germans or not). Churchill knew that it was a long process, and the outcome could be anything. He decided to burn the midnight oil, prepared a passionate speech, and delivered it in the parliament. Through this speech, he managed to convince the parliament to fight against Germany.

An excerpt of the speech goes:

"We shall go on to the end. We shall fight in France, we shall fight on the seas and oceans, we shall fight with growing confidence and growing strength in the air, and we shall defend our island, whatever the cost may be. We shall fight on the beaches; we shall fight on the landing grounds, we shall fight in the fields and the streets, we shall fight in the hills; we shall never surrender."

This speech influenced British citizens and inspired them to go to war with full energy, and we know the result.

The United States faced the worst depression in 1929; President Roosevelt played an essential role in their economic recovery. Let's find out how he used his communication skills to bring the economy back on track.

3.2 How Franklin D. Roosevelt Won the Confidence of US Citizens

The United States was suffering from the Great Depression during 1929–1933. In this period, the US's GDP fell by a whopping 30 per cent, the stock market fell by 90 per cent, and industrial production fell by 45 per cent. It was a terrible time for the US economy.

It was the year 1933, and President Roosevelt decided to address US citizens over the radio. He termed this address as 'fire-side chat.' By that time, 9 out of 10 US households had the radio. His first speech was about the 'banking crisis'. In the speech, he explained his policy to overcome the banking problem. The policy was the 'new deal'. His address to the nation was so passionate, that people trusted him and gained confidence. Within a few weeks, the economy started rebounding, and finally, the US came out of the Great Depression.

Do you know Roosevelt hosted 30 fire-side chats from 1933 to 1940? He is the only US President to win four consecutive presidential elections.

The secret of this address was that he kept the address informal, and in a conversational tone. Roosevelt used simple language, examples, and analogies in the fire-side chats to easily communicate his policies. He used to start the chats with the greeting "My friends", and referred to himself as "I", and the American citizen as "you", as if he was addressing his listeners directly and personally.

Both these examples show us how the world leaders used communication as their biggest weapon against uncertainty, and instilled confidence in their citizens.

Don't you think Roosevelt's "fire-side chat" inspired Indian prime minister, Narendra Modi, to start *"Man Ki Baat"*, which is also an informal talk on the radio?

Roosevelt even used his communication skills to persuade American citizens to support Britain in World War II. Let us find out how he did it.

3.3 Where There Is a Will, There Is a Way

During World War II, Germans had defeated the French and British army in the battle at Dunkirk in June 1940. The. British were worried about the German winning spree.

World War II had begun on September 1, 1939. Within 10 months, Germany defeated Czechoslovakia, Hungary, Austria, Denmark, the Netherlands, Belgium, Norway, and France.

As expected, the German air force started bombing London and nearby areas, pushing Britain for quick surrender. German naval forces sank British ships.

Winston Churchill wrote a desperate 15-page letter, to Franklin D. Roosevelt, to support Britain in the World War. There were not many options left with him.

Americans were not keen to join World War II. The reasons being the devastating effect of World War I and that they had just come out of the Great Depression. Americans wanted their country to stay out of the so-called European war.

The United States had passed the Neutrality Act, which prohibited selling arms to warring nations.

By 1940, Franklin Roosevelt had been president for two terms, and he was about to appear for the presidency for the third term. Historically, no other president had served for more than eight years. He wanted to help Britain, but considering the majority of Americans were against the war, he didn't reply to the letter right away. He feared backlash from his people, which would increase the chances of losing the presidential election.

During the third term presidency campaign, he had promised the American people that the country would be kept out of the war.

Few months after winning the presidential election, Franklin Roosevelt was determined to help Britain. He addressed the American people through one of his radio fire-side chats. It became famous as his "Arsenal of Democracy" speech. He started by saying, *"This is not a fire-side chat on war. It is a talk about national security...If Great Britain goes down, the axis powers (Germans), will be in a position to bring enormous military and naval resources against United States."*

Knowing that Americans were against getting involved in the war, he focused on the importance of assisting the British, who were doing the fighting and keeping the Nazi threat away from US shores. Franklin Roosevelt said, *"We are the Arsenal of Democracy. Our national policy is to keep war away from this country."* The implication was that the best way to accomplish what Roosevelt said was to send military aid to the country (Britain), which was keeping the enemy at bay.

In an address in 1939, President Roosevelt assured the nation, that he would do all he could to keep the United States out of the war. Still, at the same time, he said, "When peace has been broken anywhere, the peace of all countries everywhere is in danger."

These speeches convinced Americans, that the best way to avoid future American casualty, was to support Britain with arms and ammunition, so that the Germans were defeated without any more loss of life.

Franklin Roosevelt ended the Neutrality Act and introduced a Lend-Lease Act, through which vast amounts of warships and ammunition were given to Britain and other countries fighting against the Axis forces.

Therefore, it was effective communication that helped Roosevelt to convince his fellow citizens.

Now, coming back to the current scenario. What do sales and marketing people do to sell their products? They communicate in a way that convinces consumers to spend money and buy their products. They first identify the need, and then pitch the product according to customer needs, to close the deal in a smoother and faster way.

Do you know just the movie's name, its poster, or a book cover, can influence your decision to watch the movie or buy the book? It happens because the name, poster, or cover of the book communicates with you. Your experience leads you to form a perception and get attracted to it.

Do you know what the most used words in advertisements are? Do you know that for 30-second television advertisement content, research and planning are done for months? Every word spoken or shown in an advertisement is analysed by consumer behaviour experts to create maximum impact on targeted consumers. The most used words are: discount, new, now, hurry, more, guaranteed, hassle-free, save, improved, extra, smart, sale, and limited period offer. Sounds familiar? Doesn't it?

In your professional life, you might have observed that there is a significant weightage given to communication skills during the interview assessment process, irrespective of any job profile.

Have you ever asked yourself why companies spend time and money to communicate their vision, mission, and goal of organisation with its employees? It's done to align the employees towards a common objective. Research has proved that if employees are aligned, productivity goes up, leading to higher profitability. Thus, communication skills can affect your personal and professional life.

In the next chapter, we'll understand the power of purpose.

CHAPTER 4

THE POWER OF PURPOSE

"Thoughts lead on to purpose, purpose leads on to actions, actions form habits, habits decide character, and character fixes our destiny."

– Tryon Edwards

When we get passionate about doing something, there is no pain, no burnout, and no excuses. Ask a scientist who works 20 hours a day; he does not work this hard just to earn money, he has a mission to achieve, i.e. there is a purpose behind his work. It could be inventing vaccines to eradicate deadly diseases or the invention of affordable medicines for the poor. People normally would work for 8 to 12 hours, that too, with a lot of frustration, I am sure you might have come across people who work only for money. They constantly crib about everything in life, because they are not attached to their work.

In Japanese, the purpose of like is called *ikigai*. A study on Japanese people found that those who had a strong connection to their sense of purpose lived longer than those who didn't.

Renowned author, Dan Buettner, researched on ikigai and wrote in his book that the two most vulnerable times in a person's life are the first 12 months after birth and 12 months following retirement. You might have heard of instances in the news that perfectly healthy men have died shortly after their retirement. Researchers believe that such men lacked purpose in their lives, which affected their health. A study of retired employees of Shell Oil found that employees who retired early (aged 55) were likely to die earlier than those who retired at the age of 65.

This research indicates that while they were working, there might have been some purpose driving them. In the absence of purpose, their behaviour and nature changed, which affected not only health but also their relationships.

India's biggest FMCG company, Hindustan Unilever Limited, believes in purposes so much that they have declared three pillars which are—companies with purpose last, brands with purpose grow, and people with purpose thrive.

As Stephen Covey once said, "*If the ladder is not leaning against the right wall, every step we take just gets us to the wrong place faster.*" Therefore, purpose drives human beings, and the absence of purpose, takes away the zeal and motivation from our lives.

4.1 How Did Steve Jobs Convince John Scully to Join Apple?

In 1983, Pepsi was one of the world's leading brands and then, John Scully was its president. He was a highly successful professional. He had become the president of Pepsi in 1977, at the age of 38 years.

John Scully used to get many offers from the world's best companies, but he never thought of leaving Pepsi as he had everything, i.e. prestige, money, and motivation. He was a role model for executives, as he had started working in Pepsi as a trainee and became the president of the company.

At that time, Apple Inc. was just a startup. Steve Jobs managed the operation, but he was inexperienced. Thus, he was looking for someone who can lead Apple. He zeroed down the name of John Scully.

For John Scully, it didn't make sense to join the relatively unknown company, which was founded only 7 years ago and sold personal computers. There was no guarantee that Apple would even exist in the next few years.

Steve Jobs was determined to take John Scully on-board. He thought there were no other means that would help convince John Scully, but to tell him that his contribution to humankind would be immense if he joined the computer revolution; he simply used the "purpose" card. During Steve Jobs' meeting with John Scully, he asked, "*Do you want to sell sugar water for the rest of your life, or do you want to come with me, and change the world?*"

This single question pushed John Scully to change his future. In the same year, he left Pepsi and joined Apple computers, and the rest is history.

4.2 How Do Organisations Use Purpose to Increase Productivity?

The biggest challenge for any organisation is to motivate their disengaged employees. A disengaged employee is someone who usually does not enjoy work, constantly cribs about working conditions, and does the bare minimum job. Such employees spread negativity in their circles and push motivated employees to also disengage. In a simple sentence, they work for the sake of spending mandatory hours in the office.

To solve this sort of problem, organisations share the purpose of the company's existence. If people know that their work will help someone needy, or there is some noble cause, chances are very high that employees give their 100 per cent.

The organisation's purpose should convey its role in the broader economic, societal, and environmental context, i.e. more than just profit-making.

Some examples of organisational purpose are:

+ Merck: "Our purpose is to preserve and improve human life."

+ Apple: "To bring the best user experience to its customers through its innovative hardware, software, and services."

+ Southwest Airlines: "We connect people to what's important in their lives."

✦ Google: "To organise the world's information and make it universally accessible and useful."

✦ Microsoft: "To empower every person and every organisation on the planet to achieve more."

✦ Zappos: "Our purpose is to inspire the world by showing it's possible to simultaneously deliver happiness to customers, employees, community, vendors, and shareholders in a long-term sustainable way."

The purpose of an organisation helps employees formulate long-term direction and business strategy, it inspires innovation, increases brand trust and loyalty, and creates customer-centricity.

Research by a leading management consulting company, Gallops, proves that organisations with purpose increase productivity, retention rates, attract the best talent, and provide pride and engagement.

Have you ever wondered why millions are mobilised by the appeal of saints and honest politicians? The answer lies in their noble purpose.

You donate blood with the purpose of saving an unknown person's life.

In the next chapter, we will get to know the power of dreams, i.e., how your dreams have the power to shape your future.

———◆———

CHAPTER 5

THE POWER OF DREAMS

"Dream is not that which you see while sleeping; it is something that does not let you sleep."

– Dr. Abdul Kalam

Dreams of achieving something help align all your efforts in that direction. Dreams motivate, inspire, improve, and help you achieve any goal. Dreaming for a significant purpose is essential, and it can even change the course of your entire life.

Henry Ford said, *"Whether you think you can, or you think you can't – you are right."* Therefore, believing in your dreams is really important.

Let me share how Martin Luther King Junior inspired people against racism.

5.1 Martin Luther King, Jr. and His Dream

In the 1950s and 1960s there was a growing call for equality in the United States. African-Americans were discriminated based on their skin colour. Martin Luther King, Jr. started civil disobedience to protest against discrimination.

In 1964, he addressed the people of the USA against racism and discrimination; he used the power of a dream to inspire millions of black people.

Here's an excerpt of his famous speech:

I have a dream, that one day this nation will rise up and live out the true meaning of its creed — we hold these truths to be self-evident: that all men are created equal. I have a dream that one day, on the red hills of Georgia, the sons of former slaves and the sons of former slave-owners will be able to sit down together at a table of brotherhood. I have a dream that one day, even the state of Mississippi, a desert state, sweltering with the heat of injustice, and oppression, will be transformed into an oasis of freedom and justice. I have a dream, that my four little children, will one day live in a nation where they will not be judged by the color of their skin, but by the content of their character. I have a dream today! I have a dream that one day, down in Alabama, with its vicious racists, with its Governor having his lips dripping with the words of interposition and nullification; one day right there in Alabama little black boys and little black girls will be able to join hands with little white boys and white girls as sisters and brothers.

I have a dream today!

I have a dream, that one day every valley shall be exalted, every hill and mountain shall be made low, the rough places will be made plain, and the crooked places will be made straight, and the glory of the Lord shall be revealed, and all flesh shall see it together.

This speech from Martin Luther King, Jr. is known as one of the excellent speeches in human history.

Steve Jobs is known for his famous saying "Dream bigger", and he preached on it. He became the epitome of success with his big dreams. He perfected a blend of dedication and hard work to accomplish his dream. The initial dream of providing a computer in every person's hands is what inspired him and all of Apple.

5.2 Walt Disney and His Dream

Walt Disney had said, *"If you can dream it, you can do it."* He was a dreamer from an early age. Having said that, dreaming alone is not going to help, you also need passion.

Walt Disney did not achieve success easily. He was fired from his job of a newspaper editor because, as per his boss, "He lacked imagination and had no good ideas." When he was jobless, Disney formed an animation company, which ultimately went bankrupt. Still, it was his dream of incorporating the best amusement park, that kept pushing him, and finally, he got success.

Have you ever heard about a person who didn't have a clue about what they wanted in their life, yet they became highly successful? Of course not. The dream acts as a compass and provides the direction that we should travel towards.

We have plenty of examples of dreamers succeeding despite adverse conditions: Think of Napoleon, who despite having humble parentage, went on to become an emperor. Beethoven composed some of the most celebrated music even after losing hearing ability. The English novelist Charles Dickens was born in poverty, yet he never abandoned his dream of becoming a novelist.

Do you have a dream that does not allow you to sleep? If yes, you will achieve success in fulfilling that dream.

In the next chapter, we will go through the power of out-of-the-box thinking.

CHAPTER 6

THE POWER OF OUT-OF-THE-BOX THINKING

"Telephone did not come into existence from the persistent improvement of the postcard."

– Amit Kalantri

We know the saying "The only thing constant in life is change", i.e., change is inevitable, but we still resist it. The same stands true for the reluctance to do something differently. The reason for this reluctance is "fear of failure".

Thinking out-of-the-box is a metaphor for thinking differently, unconventionally, or forming a new perspective. This phrase often refers to novel or creative thinking.

Some people call lateral thinking out-of-the-box thinking.

Let me share some examples of how this has helped individuals and organisations succeed.

6.1 How Thinking Differently Leads to Success

You might have seen athletes who participate in high jump. For quite a long time, athletes used to believe that during the jump, the body should be upright and if one leg crosses the obstacle, the entire body will go over it. See the picture below.

In our childhood some of us might have done this kind of high jump.

Then somebody thought to do things differently and decided to cross the bar first with the head, and then mid-section, and then legs. Though it would have been awkward initially, that became the best way to do the high jump.

In 1968, the Olympic Games held in Mexico was where something extraordinary happened in the high jump. A relatively unknown athlete, Dick Fosbury, prepared to complete his first attempt at the high jump event. As a teenager, he had failed to get into his high school basketball team. Fosbury had failed in his attempts at various disciplines within athletics. He was six feet and four inches tall, hence, he chose high jump. However, he was not as successful.

Before Dick Fosbury's Olympic high jump event, athletes relied on three techniques to clear the high jump bar. They were the scissors, western roll, and a straddle jump. You can see these techniques in the picture below..

Image Source: Britannica Academic

All these three techniques had one thing in common: they were designed to allow the athlete to land safely on their feet after clearing the bar.

However, Fosbury knew that he had little chance of winning against top athletes using these techniques.

He had no choice other than innovating a new technique for competing at the highest level. He decided that rather than jumping face forward, using the conventional "straddle" technique, he would jump off the "wrong foot", arch his back, and clear the bar backwards.

Incidentally, Fosbury received heavy criticism from his coaches, and the press, for his unconventional jumping technique (the world doesn't accept changes so easily).

Reportedly, some local newspaper even called him the "World's laziest high jumper". However, such criticism didn't stop Dick Fosbury from perfecting his new "Fosbury flop" technique, which soon paid off.

Fosbury won the Olympics qualifying championship, and thus qualified for the upcoming Olympic Games in 1968, this was his opportunity to display this new high jump technique, and he did not disappoint himself.

Dick Fosbury used his "Fosbury flop" to win the gold medal, as well as to break the record. His innovation totally changed the high jump sport forever.

Within a few years after the Olympics, the "Fosbury flop" had become the conventional technique for a high jump athlete. Since then, every Olympic gold medallist, and record holder has successfully used the "Fosbury flop" technique to win high jump.

Fosbury's willingness to experiment with new ideas contributed to his success, but something else also played an important role—his environment.

Of course, Fosbury deserves an accolade for his out-of-the-box thinking, but his school also played an essential role in changing the high jump technique.

Until the early 1960s, high jump athletes used to clear the bar, and land on the hard ground or loose soil, etc. thus, all high jump techniques attempted to ensure that the athletes landed on their feet to avoid any injury.

Forbury studied in a high school, which was one of the first to install a deep foam matting for high jump landing. This cushion allowed Fosbury, to try out new ways to clear the bar, i.e., landing on his back instead of his leg.

Thus, there was no way that the "Fosbury flop" technique could have been innovated before the introduction of the foam mats—because the innovation depended on the existence of a foam mat for a soft landing. That is why, the right environment also plays an essential role in the success of a person and institution.

I hope you might have realised now why most of the Olympics medals were won by developed nations.

6.2 How Out-of-the-Box Thinking of Proctor & Gamble Employees Helped the Company

Vicks is one of the most successful products of the famous FMCG player Proctor & Gamble. Vicks was earlier categorised as allopathic medicine.

Allopathic medicine prices were not regulated in India until 1962, but considering Chinese aggression in North-east India, the government feared an increase in prices due to the shortage of medicine or drugs. This led to the control of drug prices in 1962. The act empowered the government to control and prohibit the production, supply, distribution, trade and commerce of any commodity deemed as "essential". The India-China war eventually ended, but the Drug Price Control Order (DPCO) remained. Its various iterations (including the 2013 version), defined drugs as "any pharmaceutical, chemical, biological, or plant-based product including its salts, esters, isomers, analogues and derivatives, conforming to standards specified in the Drugs and Cosmetics Act, 1940".

In 1966, the DPCO made prior approval of prices by the government mandatory to manufacture drugs. With Vicks categorized as an allopathic substance, the company couldn't increase the price, as price increase would have violated the government's DPCO.

Price and profit ceilings by government called for severe cost-cutting measures by Proctor & Gamble. To reduce production costs, the petroleum base of the product was replaced with locally sourced oils. The chemists were not happy with the low margins, and finally, in 1983, a nationwide boycott by chemists placed the company under an immense strain. The boycott was to get a higher margin.

There was no scope of price increase because of government regulation, hence, the decision to provide a higher margin would have eroded the profitability of Proctor & Gamble.

Between DPCO and the chemists' boycott, Vicks was hard-pressed for solutions. Top management of the company did many internal meetings, but no solution was found.

During one of the brainstorming sessions, an employee of P&G came up with the revolutionary idea of rebranding Vicks as an Ayurvedic product. It was a watershed moment for the history of the brand, as Ayurvedic products were not covered in the DPCO.

The DPCO applied to "pharmaceutical, chemical, biological or plant-based products" thus leaving little scope for the exception. However, to encourage indigenous, small and medium industries, and to reduce import, it excluded three types of drugs. These were "any medicines included in any bona fide Ayurvedic (including Siddha), and Unani (tibb) system of medicines; any medicine in the homeopathic system of medicines; any substance to which the provisions of the Drugs and Cosmetics Act, 1940 (23 of 1940), do not apply".

Vicks's research team corroborated its ingredients with ancient texts at the Ayurvedic library at Bombay University and claimed that Vicks was based on Ayurvedic principles. This was approved and finally, Vicks was registered as an Ayurvedic brand under the Indian system of medicine.

The benefits of being registered as an Ayurvedic brand were enormous, as these were exempt from licences, excise duty, and most importantly – price control. Being an Ayurvedic medicine, Vicks could freely be circulated in non-drug stores, which led to a huge increase in Vicks's sale.

P&G managed to solve their problem with the help of out-of-the-box thinking.

Let's go through another story of a company where the problem was of a different type.

6.3 Solutions Can Be Simple

A toothpaste factory had a typical problem. They sometimes dispatched empty toothpaste boxes without the toothpaste tube inside. Of course, it was terrible on the part of the company, as shopkeepers were sometimes getting an empty box. Realising the problem, the CEO of the company conducted a meeting with his top management. They agreed to hire an external engineering company to solve their empty boxes problem. The project followed the usual process: budget, request for proposal and third-parties' selection. After two months of hard work and spending 80 lakh rupees, they found the solution.

They solved the problem using a high-tech precision scale, which would sound a bell and flashlights whenever a toothpaste box weighed lesser than it should. The line would stop; the operator would walk over, remove the defective box, and press another button to restart the line. Because of the new package monitoring process, no empty boxes were being shipped out of the factory. The CEO was delighted to see the solution. For the next few months, he didn't receive any complaint about empty boxes.

One day, while taking rounds of the factory, the CEO went to the packing line (line responsible for putting the tube into the box) to check out the part of the line where the precision machine was installed. He observed that just ahead of the new 80 lakh rupees solution, sat a 500-rupee table fan, blowing the empty boxes off the belt and into a bin. He asked the manager what that was about.

"Oh, that," the manager replied, "actually, the operator from maintenance put this fan there because he was tired of walking over to restart the line every time the bell rang."

The CEO realised that if an empty box problem had been discussed with line operators, the company might have saved 80 lakh rupees. Nevertheless, the CEO learnt his lesson.

Asian Paints is India's largest paint manufacturer. Let's see how one of the co-founders thought out-of-the-box to penetrate the rural market.

6.4 How Asian Paints Seized the Opportunity

Champaklal H. Choksey was one of the founding members of Asian Paints. In the initial year, Asian Paints was getting very tough competition from foreign as well as Indian paint companies. During one of the village tours, Mr. Choksey observed that villagers paint the horns of their bull in a bright colour. The problem the villagers were facing was that their requirement was very less but, they had to buy the paint in a large pack. Affordability was a big challenge for poor villagers. Mr. Choksey realised the potential and launched paint in 50 to 100-millilitre pack, which no other paint makers were supplying. This helped create demand for Asian Paints in rural areas, and thus, stockists and retailers were happy to keep Asian Paints and sell it. Once the relationship between shopkeepers and Asian Paints was well established, it was much easier to penetrate further into the paint segment.

Thus, the decision to launch smaller packs helped Asian Paints grow and become India's biggest paint company.

I hope you would agree with me that out-of-the-box ideas can help individuals and companies excel.

Now let's see things differently, i.e. how some of the new business models appeared.

6.5 How Aggregator Business Works

As the world's largest taxi service provider, Uber's daily rides are 17 million in number. World's largest lodging provider, Airbnb, provides 2 million people night stays daily; and the world's largest retail and e-commerce company, Amazon, dispatches 1.3 million packages daily.

What is the common factor among all these number one players in their respective fields? They do not own the things that they sell, i.e. Uber does not own taxis, Airbnb does not own hotels, and Amazon does not own 95 per cent of the products it sells.

These companies act as aggregators i.e., they bring the service or product providers and product seekers on the same platform. The platform is online, which has no delay.

When the online platform was not available, newspapers acted as aggregators. You might have seen tonnes of Classified advertisements. Now, Classified advertisement has changed the form, and people put their offerings on the web portal, and seekers can easily find and avail their service or products.

In the first instance, out-of-the-box thinking seems illogical, as people are shy to share such ideas in public. Someone rightly said, "Most ideas are killed in the mind only because of fear." Here, fear is "what would people say?" During the brainstorming session, all ideas should be written down, without any judgements. The reason behind noting down every idea is to encourage participants to come up with all sorts of ideas, even the silly ones, as out-of-the-box ideas can't come from thinking logically in a straight line.

Do you use out-of-the-box thinking to solve your problems?

In the next chapter, we will go through the power of perseverance.

———•———

CHAPTER 7

THE POWER OF PERSEVERANCE

"Don't let your failures bring you down. Don't be a quitter; persistence is the key."

– Abraham Lincoln

Persistence is doing something despite challenges or delays in achieving success. There are difficulties in the journey of achieving bigger goals, therefore, we must have the perseverance to continue working on our goals.

In the previous chapter, you have read about the power of dreams. Most people dream, but only a few can fulfil their dreams. Martin Luther King Jr. said, *"If you can't fly then run, if you can't run then walk, if you can't walk then crawl, but whatever you do, you have to keep moving forward."*

Those who have achieved success are the ones who have the skill of perseverance.

Michael Jordan is considered the greatest basketball player the world has ever seen. He once quoted, *"I've missed more than 9,000 shots in my career. I've lost almost 300 games. 26 times, I've been trusted to take the game winning shot, and missed. I've failed over and over and over again in my life. And that is why I succeed."*

In ancient Indian texts, it's said, "Anybody can start, but those who start with the end in mind are the winners." Perseverance keeps you dedicated to your goal.

7.1 Karoly Takacs and His Perseverance for Olympic Gold

Karoly Takacs, 28, was an officer in the Hungarian army. He was considered one of the best pistol shooters in the world and it was believed that he would win the gold medal at the upcoming Olympic Games. Then one day, disaster struck. During an army training session, a hand grenade exploded in his right hand and permanently damaged it. The dream of gold was shattered. He could have gone into depression and cursed his luck. But, no. Karoly was determined to win the Olympic gold.

Rather than thinking of what he had lost, Karoly decided to focus on what he still had, the determination to succeed, the burning desire of getting the gold medal, the mental strength, and a healthy left hand.

Karoly was back on the shooting range within a month, learning to shoot with his left hand. It was not so easy; he had never shot with his left hand. The right shoulder pained, the left hand was unsteady, but he was determined. Two successive Olympics were cancelled due to World War II, and finally, the games came to London in 1958, 10 years after Karoly's accident. Karoly Takacs was chosen to represent Hungary in the shooting event.

Guess what? He won the gold, that too by shooting with his left hand.

Isn't it an amazing story of the power of perseverance?

7.2 Thomas Alva Edison's Incredible Story

When Thomas Alva Edison was a young boy, school teachers used to called him "stupid" and "unteachable". He spent his initial years working and being fired from various jobs, including termination from a telegraph company at the age of 21. Despite these failures, he never strayed from his true passion, which was inventing. His perseverance for invention led him to obtain 1,093 patents in his career. A few of his remarkable inventions are the light bulb, stock printer, phonograph, and alkaline battery. Edison claimed that he faced more failure during his career than success. Imagine how determined he was.

Edison once said, *"Genius is 1 per cent inspiration, and 99 per cent perspiration."*

Edison had become famous after inventing the light bulb, following which he wanted to invent light bulb filament, so that its affordability and quality could go up. At the time, ore mines were far away from his place and shipping costs were very high. To counter this issue, Edison opened an ore mining plant in his state. For almost a decade, Edison devoted all his time and money to the plant. He realised a lot of scope of improvement in mining operations, and hence, worked on that and obtained 47 patents for inventions designed to make the plant run more smoothly. After doing everything possible, Edison's project failed due to the low-quality ore.

Nevertheless, one of the 47 inventions in the mining plant clicked. A newly designed crushing machine revolutionised the cement industry and helped him to earn back the money he lost in failed ore mining.

Henry Ford is credited for mass production of cars, thanks to his moving assembly line concept, but do you know, Edison's ore mining project inspired it? Thus, it may be believed that Edison paved the way for modern-day industrial production.

Therefore, despite all the negative feedback and failures, Edison managed to become one of the greatest scientists.

Similarly, one more great personality faced numerous failures, but his power of perseverance helped him succeed.

7.3 Abraham Lincoln and His Failures

Abraham Lincoln faced many failures in his life. Repeated failures shatter the person, but he chose not to bow against failure. His perseverance led him to become one of the greatest US presidents of all time.

Before becoming president, he encountered several challenges. His mother died when he was just nine years; his business measurably failed; he lost state legislature election; he lost his job; he wanted to go to law school, but couldn't even get an admission; he tried starting a business and borrowed some money from his friends but by the end of the year, he faced bankruptcy. Can you imagine how tough it was for him? Still, he decided not to give up.

He contested in the election for the state legislature once again, and this time he won. Likewise, a year later, he got engaged and was about to be married. He thought everything would be right now, but then, his fiancé died, and this incident led to a nervous breakdown. He was bedridden for six months.

After recovering, he tried entering politics again and faced defeat many times. Still, he did not lose hope; he kept on doing social work and was finally elected president of the US.

Do you know somebody who faced more challenges than Abraham Lincoln did? I do not. Therefore, what was the reason for his success? Obviously many qualities, but the one that stands out is his perseverance.

7.4 Albert Einstein and Perseverance

Einstein is now known as a genius, but young Albert was not viewed as much of a bright scholar. His parents and school teachers began to think he was mentally disabled and socially awkward because he did not start to speak until the age of four nor did he read until he was seven. Einstein was eventually expelled from school and even denied entry to Zurich Polytechnic School. After education, he worked as a patent clerk, and finally, his perseverance helped him reach the pinnacle of scientific research.

The purpose of sharing all the above stories of famous personalities is to emphasise that success can be achieved despite tough challenges if there is perseverance.

If you want to taste success, be ready for difficulties; it is perseverance that will keep you moving.

In the next chapter, we will go through the power of deep diving.

———•———

CHAPTER 8

THE POWER OF DEEP DIVING

"Ideas are like fish. If you want to catch little fish, you can stay in the shallow water. But if you want to catch the big fish, you've got to go deeper."

– David Lynch

A deep dive into something is a thorough investigation and analysis of it. We take hundreds of decisions and arrive at numerous conclusions based on our experience. We face many challenges in our lives, and at the same time, we need to make suitable decisions to solve problems. To arrive at the solution, it's essential to understand the problem first. Deep diving helps in understanding and finding the solution.

You might have heard the phrase "Less knowledge is very dangerous." The synonym of less knowledge is superficial knowledge. In our fast-moving world, there is little time to understand something before we form opinions about them.

Deep diving into things can be time-taking and difficult, but it's undoubtedly a recipe for success. We often ignore this skill, because of our overconfidence.

In this chapter, I would like to share how things can be understood by going deeper into the subject.

Let's understand the importance of science and technology for a country like India.

8.1 How Lack of Innovation Can Push Prosperous Countries into Deep Poverty, and Why Science and Technology are Essential for the Developing World

As per the studies, India's GDP contribution to the world was 24 per cent in 1750, which fell to 2 per cent in 1900. Even today, it is approximately 6 per cent.

No wonder why, in good old days, India was called "the golden bird".

The same goes for China too whose contribution in 1750 was more than 30 per cent of the world's GDP.

At that time, when India and China were prospering, America was busy fighting for its independence, and Europe was going through a new reckoning due to the French revolution. Fast forward to the twenty-first century, the entire story has turned upside down, and now an average American and European is 25 times richer than an average Indian.

You might be thinking, what went wrong?

The answer lies in the fact that India and China missed the bus of the first industrial revolution. Export has been a critical component in the prosperity of any country in the world; you name any developed country today, and by default, all will be export-oriented countries. Eg. Germany, UK, China, Japan, UAE, South Korea, etc. Before the first industrial revolution, India and China dominated the world in terms of exports.

In the middle of the eighteenth century, the source of power was human labour, and almost all industries were dependent on skilled hands. India and China had an abundance of human capital, because of the higher population. Therefore, the two countries never looked for alternative power sources (wind, flowing water, etc.). On the other hand, Britain had a shortage of manpower, so they were actively looking for an alternate power source. They say "necessity is the mother of invention"; British people learnt how to harness water, wind, and steam for power generation. This gave a big boost to their industrial production, which gave them a massive advantage over other countries. Power looms outdid handlooms, and thus, India and China's textile industry suffered heavily. This was the first industrial revolution.

Europeans must get credit for this technological breakthrough, which helped them become exporters of the world. This marked the beginning of European supremacy.

The second industrial revolution was in the second half of the nineteenth century when Europeans and Americans focused on large scale production with electric motors, internal combustion engines, and even moving assembly lines. India missed this bus again, and paid heavily for being a laggard in adopting science and technology. Concisely, research and development was then the major differentiating factor between India and Western countries.

The third industrial revolution started with the advent of computers in 1959. This changed the way people used to manufacture, communicate, and analyse.

Post this, China and India's per capita income became so low, that manufacturing in these countries or outsourcing to these countries became attractive for developed countries. China seized the opportunity, by opening its economy in 1978, which helped them become the "workshop of the world" (manufacturing hub).

Finally, after one of the worst economic crises in India, the government forced to open its economy in 1991. This economy's opening helped us grow in leaps and bounds, as it infused the much-needed money, and technology in the market. Still, by then, China had advanced too much in production. Hence, despite the low manpower cost, very little scope was left for India to produce and export. Luckily, the language English, though cursed by many so-called nationalists, came to our rescue. English gave us an edge in information technology, and soon India became the "back office" of the world and the hub of IT and ITES services. This contributed to one-third of India's total exports by the late 1990s.

Recently, India has grown at 6 per cent per annum, compared to the rest of the world at 2.5 per cent, because of our USP of low manpower cost. However, this growth story is likely to come to a grinding end because of new machines.

Developed countries are at the cusp of embracing the fourth industrial revolution, which is an imminent threat. Artificial intelligence, machine learning, and mechanised workforce can easily defeat cheaper Indian manpower. Thus, India's biggest USP will be in danger. Already we are witnessing stagnation in the IT sector, because of algorithm-based technology being used by importers of IT services. Thus, for us the fourth industrial revolution is essential, and this time, India must not miss this bus.

The fourth industrial revolution has already started. It is everywhere, and right now, in your hand as well. As per Prof. Schwab, it is characterised by a fusion of technologies, blurring the lines between the physical, digital, and biological spheres. It is marked by emerging technology breakthroughs in several fields including robotics, artificial intelligence, nanotechnology, quantum computing, biotechnology, IoT, 3D printing, and autonomous vehicles. Siri by Apple and Alexa by Amazon are classic examples of machine learning. Now, these devices talk to you, and based on the historical data, they even give suggestions. Autonomous driving is almost a reality now.

For a developing country like India, the only option is to join the fourth industrial revolution bandwagon.

I hope you might have got a 360-degree view of the problem and its solution.

Let's talk about something which you noticed but never bothered to find the reason behind.

8.2 Water Is Essential for Life While Diamond Is Not, but Why Is Diamond Costlier than Water?

How is something, which is essential for life, cheaper than a non-essential item?

The answer is a complicated phrase, "the law of diminishing marginal utility". Uh oh, did that not make sense? Do not worry, I also struggled to understand it initially, let me demystify it. The higher the supply we have of something and the more we use it, the less we value it. We have oceans of water, large rivers, and huge reservoirs of groundwater, which we carelessly pump and use. We have far fewer diamonds that are hidden and buried in rocks. In simple terms, we do not respect the things that are available in adequate quantities, but we value rare things. Water is available everywhere, while diamonds are not readily available. Therefore, water has less value than diamonds. It's a game of demand and supply, i.e., if supply is more than demand, the value is less.

Let me reverse this situation, imagine a rich person with a diamond ring is lost in a jungle. He has been thirsty for hours and is about to faint or die because of dehydration when he comes across you in jungle. You are carrying one litre of water, and know from where to fetch the water. This rich person asks you for water, and you agree on the condition that you will share the water only if the rich person gives you his diamond ring. What do you think the rich man is going to do? Will he think about whether or not he should give his two-lakh-rupee diamond ring for 20 rupee worth of water? Or would he gladly offer his diamond ring and take the water? Or would he gladly offer his diamond ring and take water? Of course, he will choose water, which is supposed to be much cheaper. Hence, the cost of any product depends on demand and supply.

Let me explain this theory slightly differently. A labourer works in scorching summers and gets paid the least, while a CEO working on laptops in an AC cabin is paid the highest. The reason is demand and supply. The job of a labourer is not rare in nature, and many people are ready to do the same, and hence, they are not paid much, while the job of a CEO is very technical in nature, where not many talented people are available, hence, the salary is many times more than a labourer.

Now, I hope you understand the concept of demand and supply. Are you among the high-demand profiles or high-supply profiles? If it's high supply, upskill immediately, otherwise, things will be difficult.

8.3 Do Nature and Ancient Humans Play a Role in Your Success?

Today, you are reading this book at your own comfort. I don't think you are worried about the attack of any wild animal, or being drenched in heavy rain, or collecting wood for cooking food right now, which primitive humans used to do. I am telling this because, as humans, we have gone through a lot of challenges, but it's innovation that helps us, and today we are in the best shape. Let us go through human evolution in chronological order:

- ✦ According to the Big Bang Theory, our solar system formed 13.8 billion years ago.

- ✦ Earth came into existence around 4.5 billion years ago.

- ✦ First form of life, as a unicellular organism, emerged 3 billion years ago.

- ✦ Multicellular organism (sexual reproduction) emerged 1 billion years ago.

- ✦ Dinosaurs appeared 240 million years ago.

- ✦ Monkeys appeared 30 million years ago.

- ✦ Apes appeared almost 10 million years ago.

- ✦ Humans appeared (Homo habilis), evolved from Ape, almost 2.5 million years ago.

- ✦ Humans learnt the art of producing fire 1.5 million years ago.

- ✦ Homo sapiens appeared (wise human) 0.3 million years ago.

- ✦ Humans started agriculture 12,000 years ago.

- ✦ Humans started using metal (copper) 11,000 years ago.

- ✦ Civilisation started 6,000 years ago.

✦ Kingdoms started 4,000 years ago.

✦ Use of paper started 2,100 years ago.

✦ Use of windmills started 1,400 years ago.

✦ Humans started using "zero" in calculation 1,100 years ago.

✦ The magnetic compass was invented 900 years ago.

✦ Explosive bombs were invented 800 years ago.

✦ The printing press was invented 600 years ago.

✦ Telescope and microscope were invented 400 years ago.

✦ The steam engine was invented 250 years ago.

✦ Electricity was produced 220 years ago.

✦ The mechanical computer was invented 200 years ago.

✦ Plastic was invented 150 years ago.

✦ The modern telephone was invented 145 years ago.

✦ The light bulb was invented 140 years ago.

✦ The modern automobile was invented 134 years ago.

✦ Wireless communication with radio waves was invented 125 years ago.

✦ Television was invented 93 years ago.

✦ The personal computer was invented 63 years ago.

✦ The first artificial satellite was launched 63 years ago.

✦ The first time humans travelled to space was 59 years ago.

✦ The mobile phone came into existence 36 years ago.

✦ The internet appeared 30 years ago.

✦ Facebook appeared 16 years ago.

✦ Instagram appeared 10 years ago.

✦ TikTok appeared 3.5 years ago.

✦ 5G telecommunication trials started 2 years ago.

✦ Coronavirus spread to the world just few years ago.

✦ You are reading this book "now".

Therefore, in your success, 3 billion years of evolution plays a role!

In a nutshell, we are in comfort because of the relentless efforts of many generations.

The purpose of sharing the chronology above is to understand the importance of the work done by many unknown people before us.

OK, since we are talking about chronology, let us go through another one.

8.4 Timeline of Automobile Invention

In the last 150 years, one of the greatest inventions which has helped humankind is the invention of modern automobiles. However, as they say, "What you see is the tip of the iceberg, but what is not visible is huge base underwater", similarly, in any success, there is a long list of efforts.

In the below-mentioned chronology, you will realise how the modern car was invented.

+ 1335 – Dutchman Guido von Vigevano drew sketches of a Windwagen (wind power-driven vehicle) but not much success was achieved. It had the three key parts of a modern car: an engine (spinning windmill sails), a set of wheels and gear. It was supposed to be wind-power drive, but that could not be accomplished.

+ 1478 – Leonardo da Vinci invented the self-propelled car. However, the car remained a sketch on paper, and was never actually made. It was not exactly like a car but similar to a cart and had no seat.

+ 1769 – Nicolas-Joseph Cugnot built the first self-propelled road vehicle (steam-powered) in France. It was a three-wheeled tractor made for the French army, with a maximum speed of about two and a half miles per hour.

+ 1789 – Oliver Evans, an American, received the first US patent for a steam-powered land vehicle.

+ 1801 – Richard Trevithick, a British inventor, built a steam-powered road carriage. It is considered the first tramway locomotive designed for use on road, not railroad.

✦ 1807 – Francois Isaac de Rivaz, a Swiss inventor, built an internal combustion engine, which used a mixture of hydrogen and oxygen. He also designed a car for the engine, the first automobile powered by internal combustion. Unfortunately, it was unsuccessful.

✦ 1823 – British engineer, Samuel Brown, invented an internal combustion engine with separate combustion and working cylinders.

✦ 1832 – Robert Anderson invented the first crude non-rechargeable electric carriage in Scotland.

✦ 1863 – Belgian engineer, Jean-Joseph-Etienne Lenoir, invented the "horseless carriage", with an internal combustion engine and capable of speeding up to three miles per hour. This was the first commercially successful internal combustion engine.

✦ 1867 – German engineer, Nicolaus August Otto, improved on the internal combustion engine. His engine was the first to burn fuel directly and efficiently in a piston chamber.

✦ 1870 – Julius Hock, of Vienna, built the first internal combustion engine running on petrol.

✦ 1877 – Nicolaus Otto built the four-cycle internal combustion engine (similar engine is used today in our cars).

+ August 21, 1879 – American inventor, George Baldwin, filed the first US patent for an automobile. This invention was similar to a wagon with an internal combustion engine.

+ 1885 – German engine designer, Karl Benz, built the first true automobile powered petrol engine vehicle. It had three wheels and looked quite similar to a carriage. Karl Benz patented new technology and was therefore called "father of the modern automobile".

+ 1886 – In Michigan, Henry Ford built his first automobile.

+ 1886 – Gottlieb Wilhelm Daimler and Wilhelm Maybach invented the first four-wheeled, four-stroke engine in Germany.

+ 1893 – Brothers Frank and Charles Edgar Duryea invented the first successful gas-powered car in the United States.

+ 1895 – George Baldwin Selden, an American inventor and engineer, invented a combined internal combustion engine with a carriage. It was never manufactured.

+ 1896 – The Duryea brothers started the first American car manufacturing company in Springfield, Massachusetts. It was called Motor Wagons.

+ 1900 – A steering wheel is designed to replace the steering tiller.

✦ 1906 – Alabama sets a state maximum speed limit of eight miles per hour, i.e., 12.5 kms per hour.

✦ 1913 – "Ford Model T" production rockets from 7.5 cars per hour to 146 cars per hour, thanks to the assembly line's utilisation.

✦ 1924 – The car radio introduced.

✦ 1940 – The first four-wheel drive, all-purpose vehicle designed for the US Military. It was known as the Jeep.

✦ 1956 – The Interstate Highway Act creates a highways network which connects all parts of the United States.

✦ 1962 – Wisconsin became the first state to create a seat belt law.

✦ 1974 – Airbags become a new car safety option.

✦ 1995 – The Global Positioning System or GPS is introduced.

✦ 2001 – Hands-free bluetooth is introduced in cars.

✦ 2003 – Automatic parking capability is introduced.

✦ 2004 – LED headlamps was introduced.

Hope you would agree with the fact that a lot of work has been done in the field of automobiles, and the features you are enjoying in your car were invented by many inventors.

It's a perfect example of continuous improvement.

The automobile engine works on the principle of compression, i.e., fossil fuel is injected with pressure and it's compressed by a piston to create high temperatures to burn the fuel, i.e., fire; energy is thus released that pushes the piston.

Therefore, it is the fire in the cylinder, which rotates piston, and in turn, crankshaft, gear, and the wheels of the car.

Thus, fire is at the heart of a car's petrol or diesel engine and subsequently, the car's movement. Let us understand how fire helped humans in a real way.

8.5 How Fire Helped Humankind

An uncontrolled fire can lead to devastation, at the same time, a controlled fire can lead to prosperity. The same goes for our every act "anything in excess is bad". Now let us go back to our topic again.

Fire helped early humans protect themselves from dangerous animals. It helped them see in the night and provided warmth in the winter. Later on, fire helped humans to forge steel, and we know how steel has changed our lives. Fire helped us pasteurise milk, impacted our mobility in a big way, and the steam engine led to a mass movement. Do you know the car you use, i.e. if it's a diesel or petrol car, is run by burning the fossil fuel inside the engine cylinder? Not only this, but half of the world's electricity is also produced by burning coal. Thus, fire helped humans excel in every possible way, but the most important contribution of fire is making humans wise.

Yes, you read it right, fire helped humans become wise!

Cooking vegetables or meat killed most of the harmful germs, which helped reduce the human mortality rate. This is important because cooked food led to humans being healthier and living longer.

The most significant part is that cooking made food softer and helped digest it easily.

Hence, early humans didn't need to spend hours chewing, tearing, and digesting meat or food. This led to the decrease in muscle strength, shorter intestine, and most importantly, the development of a bigger brain. Almost all the bodily energy, which was earlier being used for muscle development and digestion was then diverted to the brain. That is why humans have the biggest brains than any other species of mammals. Research shows that the human brain consumes around 25 per cent of our energy. Therefore, the human brain developed because of the invention of fire. Further, humans invented or found more ways to make their life easier and better. This further helped save more energy available for the brain.

Had some other animals discovered fire before humans, who knows what the world might look like now?

Maybe humans might not have survived, and if they survived, then they would have been locked away in some zoo for someone's amusement.

You might have come across the phrase, *"Courage is man's surest weapon in danger."* Do you want to know how courage plays a role in sports?

Let's understand it from the example of cricket.

8.6 Why Is Courage Important?

In cricket, a spinner does flighted delivery. This means he throws with a loop so that ball spends more time in the air, and after landing on pitch, the ball turns. With the help of the turn, he beats the batsman and takes a wicket, but the irony here is that the batsman gets more time to read the ball, and can play a lofted shot for a six. Therefore, the dilemma the bowler is that if he wants a wicket, he has to be mentally prepared for it to be costly.

The second option with a spinner is to deliver faster, with no loop and less turn. This will not allow the batsman to hit a six, but then the chances of taking a wicket would be reduced.

In a test match, spinners bowl flighted balls, as taking a wicket is important, but in T20, spinners bowl a straight ball to avoid giving runs, as in T20 saving runs is more important than taking a wicket.

The real problem comes in ODIs, as both taking a wicket and saving runs are equally important. In ODIs, spinners first bowl flighted balls, and if the batsman is in an aggressive mood, he hits a few boundaries. The spinners who do not want to be costly, start bowling straight ball, and do not take any wicket. The courageous spinners take a risk and keep bowling flighted balls, and get rewarded by taking a wicket. Thus, courage helps people who take risks.

8.7 Only Looking at Trends Can Make the Forecast Go Wrong

As a result of the first and second industrial revolution, the Western world had become wealthy in the 1950s. Better lifestyle had led to more demand for shoes, clothes, toys, etc. Producing these items in Western countries was costly, as the salary of workers was high.

Therefore, the solution was to produce household goods in countries where manpower labour was cheap. Japan was reeling under poverty, and labour rate was cheaper. Hence, Japan grabbed the opportunity and started the production of household items in bulk. This led to relative prosperity in Japan, but because of that, daily wages had gone up; hence, industrialists started looking for countries with cheap labour again. South Korea got the manufacturing job, and again, because of higher economic activities, they developed, and thus, daily wages went up. Once again, product manufactures started looking for cheaper labour countries. This time China grabbed the opportunity. Because of this, China became the production hub of the world. Owing to mass production, China also got prosperous, pushing daily wages to go up. Now, industrialists choose Thailand, Vietnam, Philippines, and Bangladesh. It's certain that sooner or later, daily wages in these countries would go up. Once the salary goes up, it puts pressure to shift to lower-wage countries.

Which country, do you think, will sieze the opportunity?

Looking at the trend, your answer would be sub-Saharan countries. If this is the answer, then you are wrong. Robotics and artificial intelligence will reduce the production cost in the developed world, and manufacturing would be possible at a much cheaper price in the developed countries. So, there is no reason why production would shift further to low-wage countries. Therefore, one should never conclude without looking at all the parameters.

8.8 Don't Reach a Conclusion in Haste

Until recently, women were not allowed to work at night.

This was because of a law made by the British during their rule in India. Therefore, anybody after listening about such an Act in the twenty-first century would think that the British were against women rights, and were doing grave injustice to womenfolk. The good news is that recently this law has been amended so that women can work at night too.

Today we have electricity, i.e., street light, CCTV camera, police, mobile phone, public transport, cars, as well as, enough population, so any woman going from her workplace to her house can feel safe, but 100 years back, the scenario was very different.

100 years back, women workers travelling from their workplace to their residence in the night were vulnerable to anti-social elements. Thus, the solution was ending daily work hours of women before sunset for their safety.

Therefore, if the context is not known, chances are high that there can be a wrong interpretation.

Sometimes, if we see things from a different perspective, we can learn something entirely new. Let me share a beautiful analogy.

8.9 How Is the Brake Helpful in Driving?

If I ask you, how a brake is helpful in driving, your obvious answer will be, "The brake helps us to stop or slow down the car."

There is nothing wrong with your answer, but it's not an entirely correct answer. The biggest use of a brake is to allow you to drive the car at a high speed. I guess you might have gotten confused. Okay, let me ask another question, assume your car does not have brakes, now can you drive the car fast? No, because then, you would have an accident. So, the brake helps you drive fast, without worrying about any accidents.

At various stages in life, we find our parents, teachers, mentors, well-wishers and friends questioning our plan, direction, decision, and strategy.

We often get irritated and consider such questions as "brakes" to our plan.

However, just remember, it's because of such questions (brakes), that we have managed to reach where we are today. Without them, we could have met with an unfortunate accident.

We should be deeply and sincerely grateful to all our priceless *brakes*.

Appreciate the "brakes" in your life; without them, we would not be where we are today.

Therefore, what you see and feel has a much deeper meaning.

If you know the meaning, you will respect and value it more.

8.10 Don't Believe in Data Alone

During World War II, the Germans were shooting down the British fighter planes. British engineers thought to put extra armour cladding on some parts of the plane, so that even if an enemy's bullet hits the plane, it would survive and return to the base safely. Why did they only focus on some parts? Because, if they had chosen to put armour on the entire body, the weight would have increased considerably, affecting the fighter plane's capabilities. Therefore, researchers at the Centre for Naval Analysis were a given task—to find out the parts of the plane where armour cladding was required the most. Whenever a fighter plane used to come back from the enemy's area, the researchers noted every bullet hole and its damages on the plane's body.

As per the data, most damage was done to the wings, and tail of the plane.

The solution to their problem was simple, it was to put the armour on the plane's wings and tail. Why?

Because the data clearly showed that those were the parts where the maximum number of bullets had been fired.

However, there was a mistake. The analysis was wrong. The researchers had only looked at fighter planes that had returned to base.

Missing from the data were the planes which never came to base, i.e., those that were shot down in the enemy's area. This meant that the data showed the parts of the planes with least damages (hit by a bullet). Therefore, armoured cladding was supposed to be on the cockpit and engine instead.

We make similar mistakes in our life also we take feedback only from those who like us, and hence, chances are very high that they might not see anything wrong with you. Whereas, if you talk to someone who knows you but is not very close to you, their feedback might help you more.

My close friend started a business of a retail store just outside the city's limit. His business outlook was based on customers who used to visit his shop because he used to interact with them, but at the same time, there were many more prospective customers who were not visiting his shop. He never knew why such customers were not coming.

He was desperate to grow his business, and he asked his existing customers for suggestions to improve. The suggestions he received were to add more variety to the store and advertise about the shop so that more people grow aware of it. My friend immediately acted and added more items and put a hoarding in the city. He was very confident, because he had surveyed his existing customers, and acted accordingly but unfortunately, he was not successful.

He was frustrated. One day, he narrated the entire episode to me and asked for support. I asked him where his employees resided. He informed me that most of the employees lived in the city and they commute to work in their own vehicle. I told him to give each employee the responsibility to check with their neighbours as to why they were not shopping from his store.

He asked his employees to do the same, and after a week, he compiled the responses. The reason why his employees' neighbours were not coming to shop was because of the lack of parking facilities and high-cost perception. Therefore, this was the main reason. The customers who used to come to his shop were using public transport, hence, they never complained. My friend worked on providing valet parking and announced sales through the hoardings which he had taken, and soon customer footfall increased.

Therefore, the survey should include the "planes", which are coming to you as well as those that are not coming to you, otherwise, the analysis would be wrong.

In this chapter, you have gone through more than a dozen stories and chronologies, each detailed and proved that if deep diving is done in any subject, more meaning can be drawn from it.

This skill helps in a strategic role, which is important in top management.

Thus, if you want to be in top management in your favourite company, you have to develop the ability to deep dive.

Next chapter is about prediction skill, i.e., the ability to foresee the future.

CHAPTER 9

THE POWER OF PREDICTION

"Prediction is not just one of the things your brain does. It is the primary function of the neo-cortex, and the foundation of intelligence."

– Jeff Hawkins

A prediction or forecast is a statement about a future event. They are often, but not always, based upon experience or knowledge.

Those who forecast accurately earn respect from all, that's why we respect scientists because they work on new technology and they are the closest to know what the future could look like. In the same way politicians, CEOs, and coaches can be visionaries. People follow them because they know and understand the future much better than a common man.

The ability to predict the future comes from past experience and from assessing the current situation. If you are successful in deriving trend, you will be very close to predicting the next course of action. For example, if you know Rafael Nadal has won 12 Grand Slams on a clay court, you can guess that he might win his match if it is being played at clay court. Before the match, you will predict and tell your friend that Rafael Nadal is going to win. After that match, your friend, who does not follow tennis too much, would be surprised that your prediction has come true. For him it would be puzzling how you forecasted so accurately, but you know it was a no-brainer. Therefore, if you know statistics, i.e., past record, current form, it's possible for you to forecast.

Similarly, visionaries predict the future and many of us get surprised.

In cricket, bowlers predict the batsman's next shot and bowl accordingly. The batsman predicts the next ball from the bowlers. The success of bowlers and batsman depends on their ability to correctly predict.

In football, during counter-strike, the opponent team's defender predicts if the striker will give a pass to his colleague or move towards the goal post keeping the ball with him. Accordingly, the defender will intercept the opponent.

Therefore, it's very clear from both the examples, that apart from your talent, your ability to predict helps you to succeed.

A politician predicts the next move of his opponent, he also gauges the mood of a citizen. A student predicts the pattern of his exam paper and prepares accordingly.

For prediction, you have to be experienced. To be experienced, you have to be a keen observer. Therefore, your power of observation plays a role in your ability to predict or forecast.

A real estate developer predicts the next happening place and invests in that place. Of course, there would be a lot of research behind his prediction: like what is the plan of infrastructure development by the government, availability of water and conveyance, existing educational institutions, etc.

In previous chapters, we have discussed why CEOs are paid multiple times more than a labourer. In any company, the job of a CEO is to give direction to the organisation and sail it to safe waters, navigating the turbulent market of uncertainties. One of their key roles is to predict the future.

Let me share the story of PepsiCo, where the CEO accurately predicted the future and took a decision accordingly.

9.1 How Indira Nooyi Changed the Course of PepsiCo

PepsiCo was doing well when Indira Nooyi took over as CEO in 2008. As usual, PepsiCo board members were asking for more revenue and return. Her choices were to put more money in the marketing of existing products or to put more money into R&D.

Putting money in marketing would have given quick return while putting money in R&D would have given return only in the long-term. The existing Pepsi products were unhealthy. Indira Nooyi had observed a trend that customers are shifting towards healthy drinks and snacks.

So, if she would have put more money on marketing the existing unhealthy products, in the short term, there could have been high profitability and she would make board members happier. But, in the long-term, PepsiCo would have suffered hugely.

Indira Nooyi took the bold decision of spending money on R&D of low-calorie food products and launched a slew of healthy products. Due to this strategy, Pepsi did extremely well, and Indira Nooyi succeeded.

Here, Indira Nooyi's ability to predict the customer consumption pattern in the future helped her to excel in life, and helped her organisation become strong.

9.2 How MNCs' Inability to Predict the Future Led to Failure

George Eastman and Henry A. Strong founded Kodak, in 1888. Kodak went on to become a dominant player in the photographic film market for most of the twentieth century. Steve Sasson, the Kodak research engineer invented the first digital camera in 1975. Obviously being digital, it was filmless photography which confused Kodak's senior management, because Kodak was earning a lot of money through photographic film. This obsession led to missing out on seeing the big picture of the digital revolution. Kodak decided to put a digital camera in the cold box, and finally filed for bankruptcy in 2012.

The Finnish company, Nokia, was founded in 1865. In the late 1990s and early 2000s, Nokia was the global leader in mobile phones. I am sure you might have used a Nokia phone. Nokia was more focused on hardware, rather than software, while consumers were interested in the latter. The company was overconfident about their brand and believed they could arrive late in the smartphone game and succeed. Android swept the market, and by the time Nokia's management caught up, it was too late. Consequently, Nokia had to sell its mobile manufacturing division to Microsoft in 2013.

In colloquial language, photocopying is sometimes called "Xerox". Do you know Xerox was first to invent the personal computer? Their product was much ahead of its time. Unfortunately, Xerox's top management thought there might not be enough market for personal computers, so, they kept their focus on copy machines. Today we know how wrong they were.

National Geographic magazine started publishing in 1888. The magazine became very popular because of superior visual storytelling, and it inspired photographers and filmmakers worldwide. In the 1980s, some of the producers approached National Geographic to start a cable channel. National Geographic's management thought a cable channel would never beat a magazine, so they denied the offer. The same producer later launched the Discovery and History Channel. Finally looking at their success, National Geographic decided to launch their own cable channel in 1997, but it proved to be too late.

9.3 Creative Destruction

According to Hindu mythology, the three gods are known as Brahma - the creator, Vishnu - the preserver, and Shiva - the destroyer.

We know the term creator and preserver are positive words, but destroyer seems to be negative. But, it is not, because you cannot bring something new without removing the old.

This philosophy held true thousands of years back and applies in the contemporary world too.

Let's understand this in the economic sense, because that touches our lives the most.

The Austrian economist, Joseph Schumpeter, coined the term "creative destruction" in the 1940s. He claimed that creative destruction happened during the industrial revolution when machines pushed out craft and artisan production.

The automobile destroyed the horse and other animal-led transportation industry, making buggy makers and horse trainers redundant. Therefore, on first look, it may seem that the destruction was bad. But once many new jobs were created in car factories, car repair shops, road, and bridge construction, people started admiring the automobiles. Similarly, in the nienteenth century, when many textile workers lost their jobs to mechanised looms, there were riots in the city, and mechanised looms were blamed for job losses, but later on, when society got prosperous because of the increased productivity, there were many first-of-its-kind jobs created.

People thought that machines were ruining lives of artisans, but it was proved that machines produced more jobs and brought prosperity.

Now, fast forward to 150 years later, we are worried about job losses again, and this time it's because of artificial intelligence, robotics and blockchain.

There are numerous examples of disruption because of these technologies:

+ Netflix and Amazon Prime are casting doubt on the future of traditional television programme makers.

+ 3D printing would disrupt the manufacturing industry, and reduce the importance of logistics and inventory management.

+ Online news portals would soon end newspapers.

+ Language translation, dictation, and proofreading are being done by software, hence, eliminating the role of human support.

+ Online bookshop portals like Amazon, have forced brick-and-mortar booksellers to go out of business.

+ Payment gateways like Paytm and Google Pay are reducing the need for human bank tellers and even ATMs.

- ✦ Autonomous vehicles would eliminate the need for taxi and truck drivers.

- ✦ Airbnb and Oyo are challenging established hotel chains for their existence.

- ✦ FASTag (RFID) technology is being used in making toll payments directly, thus, eliminating the need for toll-booth attendants.

- ✦ Today software decides your cost of flight ticket as well as Uber ride fare.

- ✦ Software decides if you are a robot or not, i.e., machines are asking humans to prove that they are humans.

- ✦ Travel websites such as MakeMyTrip, Expedia, and Yatra have eliminated the need for human travel agents.

- ✦ Free online brokerage service providers like Robinhood are pushing stockbrokers and advisors to go out of business.

Of course, prima facie, it looks like there would be an avalanche of job losses, but before concluding this, we need to keep in mind that we faced similar challenges during the industrial revolution and the concerns proved to be wrong.

In 1870, 50 per cent of Americans were in the farming occupation, and today less than 2.5 per cent are. Yet, more food and agricultural production is happening than ever, and the credit goes to automation in the field of agriculture.

Do you know, currently whatever job you are doing, or whatever is the source of earning you have, there is an 80 per cent chance that it was almost non-existent just 100 years back? The whole gamut of IT, automobile, electronic manufacturing, medical equipment industry came to existence, in the true sense, in less than 100 years ago. These new industries generated millions of jobs, which nobody might have envisaged.

Someone rightly said, *"Humans were never stronger and faster than a horse, but humans decided to control it, and used it to travel faster."* Similarly, humans would control the new technology and put it to the use of improving lives.

Therefore, "creative destruction" is unavoidable, but we have to have faith that something bigger and better is on the way.

Now, let us discuss a trend. If we are able to understand it, we can predict many things in future.

9.4 The World Is Bringing Things Closer to You

Hundreds of years back, ice was being harvested in cold countries with frozen lakes. Ice blocks were transported to the cities on horse carts. Looking at the high demand for ice, scientists developed a refrigeration system, but they used to be huge, so ice factories were built in the cities. Still, the demand was high and scientists invented a household refrigerator, which helped people get ice in their kitchen whenever they wanted.

Therefore, from thousands of kilometres away, ice is now available in our kitchens. Earlier, for cooking, wood was collected from the jungle, and then some business-minded people started collecting the wood from jungle and selling it in the cities and people started purchasing wood from the market. Then, the LPG cylinder came which was supposed to be collected from the LPG distributor, then the LPG cylinders started coming to our house, and now, gas is being delivered to us through a pipe.

Earlier, people needed to go to another city to watch a movie. Looking at the demand, movie halls were made available in many cities. Soon, televisions helped us get entertainment on demand in our own house, but we were still required to travel from the bedroom to the dining room. Finally, this problem was solved by our mobile phones.

Earlier, we brought water from the river or pond, which used to be many kilometres away. Wells were dug out in the village, which shortened the distance we had to travel, but still, it was some distance away from our house. The solution was introduced as a hand pump. Now, we get water through a water pipeline to our house.

What about money? Of course, money has also moved closer to you; first the bank came to your city, then ATM came to your vicinity, and now you can do mobile transactions.

Obviously, you might have realised that whatever you want desperately, comes near you.

Therefore, if you want to become an entrepreneur, you can explore what is that distant thing which we need, and can be brought closer to us. Now, as I have given your million-dollar recipe, go ahead and conquer the world. If something can stop you, it is your fear and ignorance.

All the best!

EPILOGUE

As we draw the final curtain on our exploration of the power of ignored skills, it's worth reflecting on the journey we've taken together. Examining the small, seemingly insignificant skills we ignore every day and the profound impact they have on the trajectory of our lives, we have uncovered their power.

"Ehh, It should have been a four-page article instead of a book"—have you ever had this thought after turning the last page of any book?

If yes, trust me, my friend, you are not alone.

In this book, I've deliberately avoided the common trap of stretching simple ideas into lengthy narratives. Instead, I've condensed what could have been a 400-page book into a more accessible volume of around 150 pages.

My goal is to respect your time while delivering impactful information, to enable a more engaging and focused reading experience. Ultimately, I aim to provide you, *the reader*, a valuable resource that maximizes your learning in minimal time, empowering you to grow despite your busy schedules.

After finishing the last chapter, you may think that you already knew many of the ignored skills mentioned in the book and you may rue the fact that you never actively worked to improve yourself.

I did a deep dive to find why out individuals often fail to actively work on improving important skills despite being aware of their significance. Let me share the key reasons.

In today's fast-paced world, it is all too common to feel overwhelmed by the multitude of commitments and responsibilities vying for our attention. The demands of work, family and social obligations often leave little to no time and energy for personal development. Despite recognizing the importance of honing certain skills, we may find ourselves prioritizing immediate tasks over long-term growth, perpetuating a cycle of neglect.

I hope you agree with me.

Don't we say let me start tomorrow? In reality, tomorrow conveys today's inaction.

The question arises as to why this happens despite the resolution of doing something new. One of the key challenges we face is the lack of clear prioritization.

Though we understand the value of specific skills, we struggle to allocate the necessary attention and resources to cultivate them. Without a well-defined plan or sense of direction, important areas for improvement can easily be sidelined in favour of immediate gratification.

This lack of effective prioritization can lead to a sense of stagnation, where opportunities for growth are repeatedly overlooked amidst the clamour of daily life.

Sometimes, the fear of the unknown kicks in. The absence of knowledge or guidance on effective techniques for skill development can present a formidable barrier. This gap in understanding can breed frustration and disillusionment, further compounding our tendency to neglect personal development.

As briefly touched upon earlier, psychological barriers such as procrastination and overconfidence can significantly hinder our growth. Procrastination, fuelled by fear of failure or perfectionism, often leads us to indefinitely postpone acting on our goals. Overconfidence can blind us to our weaknesses, preventing us from acknowledging the areas where we most need improvement.

Habits and comfort zones can really put a damper on trying to learn new concepts. Let's break it down: You know when you've been doing something a certain way for a long time, it becomes almost automatic? That's a habit. So, when you're trying to learn something new, those old habits can make it super hard to switch gears. If you're used to zoning out during conversations, it can be tough to start listening actively and to engage with what someone is saying.

Now, about comfort zones—think of them like your safe space, where everything feels familiar and easy. But here's the thing: sticking to what's comfortable can hold you back big time. When you're faced with learning something new, it's tempting to stay in your comfort zone instead of taking a risk and trying something different. But playing it safe means you might miss out on cool opportunities to grow and learn new skills.

To make matters trickier, habits and comfort zones team up to keep you stuck in a rut. Your habits often coincide with your comfort zone, making it even harder to break free. So, if you're used to avoiding situations that challenge you or you prefer hanging out in places where you feel totally at ease, it's like a double whammy that keeps you from branching out and trying new things.

And let's not forget about the fear of failure. It's a big one. When you're learning something new, it's natural to worry about messing up or not being good enough. That fear can stop you dead in your tracks, making it challenging to dive into learning and take risks. But here's the secret: making mistakes is part of the learning process, and facing that fear head-on is the first step in breaking free from those habits and comfort zones. So, don't let the fear hold you back. Embrace the challenge, push yourself out of your comfort zone and keep on learning and growing!

Addressing these challenges requires a deep level of self-awareness and a willingness to confront our ingrained habits and beliefs. By actively challenging the barriers that stand in our way, we can unlock our full potential and embark on a journey of continuous growth and self-discovery. Through intentional reflection, prioritization and a commitment to learning and development, we can overcome the obstacles that have hindered our progress and realize our aspirations for personal and professional fulfilment.

If you ask me one common trait of a successful person who learns a new skill very quickly, then apart from their natural talent, the true answer is their *curiosity*.

Let me explain.

Curiosity is the fuel that powers your learning engine. It's what makes you want to explore new things, discover cool stuff and grow as a person. When you're curious, you're always itching to find out more, to try new ideas and take on challenges you've never faced before. It is that natural curiosity that pushes you to ask questions, seek answers, and push yourself to learn and grow.

Think of curiosity as your learning superpower. It gives you the drive to keep going even when things get tough, to view setbacks as opportunities to learn and improve and to think outside the box when solving problems. This mindset not only helps you bounce back from challenges but also makes you more adaptable and innovative in any situation.

Additionally, curiosity makes learning fun as it adds a sense of wonder and excitement to the process, making you eager to dive deeper into your interests and uncover new insights along the way.

Embrace your curiosity and let it guide you on a journey of discovery that will not only boost your skills and knowledge but also bring more meaning and fulfilment to your life.

When scientists are curious, they get creative, think outside the box and try new ways to figure things out.

And even when things don't go as planned, curiosity keeps them going, pushing them to learn from mistakes and to keep searching for answers. In fact, curiosity brings scientists together from different fields, helping them share research and ideas to make big discoveries. Curiosity drives scientists to push the boundaries of what we know and come up with awesome new technologies and solutions to make the world a better place.

Elon Musk, the CEO of SpaceX and Tesla, epitomizes how curiosity fuels success in leadership. His relentless curiosity and bold questioning have driven groundbreaking innovations in industries like space exploration and electric vehicles. Musk's insatiable quest for answers and willingness to challenge norms led to the founding of SpaceX, aimed at revolutionizing space transportation and enabling human colonization of other planets.

Similarly, his curiosity about sustainable energy and transportation prompted the establishment of Tesla, transforming the automotive industry with high-performance electric vehicles. Musk's curiosity not only fuels his own growth but also inspires others to join him in pursuing audacious goals, making him a transformative leader whose innovations shape the future of technology and humanity.

Therefore, I always recommend everyone to be curious. Your mobile phone is akin to a supercomputer which can provide you all the information, provided you ask for it.

Let me share what you can do to ignite curiosity.

Start by keeping an open mind and being eager to explore the world around you. Be curious about everything—from the wonders of nature to how people think and behave. Try to approach each day with a sense of wonder, like you're on a mission to uncover something fascinating. Surround yourself with different cultures, ideas and experiences to broaden your horizons and spark new interests.

To nurture your curiosity, dive into things that catch your attention. Read interesting articles, listen to cool podcasts or watch documentaries that make you go, 'Wow, I want to know more!' Don't be afraid to ask questions and dig deeper into topics that intrigue you. Whether it's experimenting with a new hobby or delving into a subject you've always wondered about, curiosity is all about taking initiative and being excited to learn. So, stay curious, explore and let your imagination run wild!

Embrace the power of curiosity by daring to ask questions, even if it means risking looking foolish. It's the willingness to inquire and seek understanding that leads to wisdom and growth. By asking questions, you open the door to new knowledge and insights, enriching your understanding of the world around you. Conversely, choosing not to ask questions out of fear of appearing foolish may result in missed opportunities for learning and personal development, ultimately perpetuating a state of ignorance. So, don't let pride or hesitation hold you back—embrace curiosity, ask questions and embark on a journey of continual discovery and enlightenment.

Think of your curiosity as your personal treasure map to knowledge. The more curious you are, the more you explore, discover and learn. And guess what? All the knowledge you gather becomes your superpower.

It is like having a secret weapon that helps you understand the world better and take smarter decisions. The more you know, the more you can see things from different angles and figure out the best path forward. So, keep feeding your curiosity, keep learning. Knowledge is your greatest asset—it is what guides you through life's twists and turns and helps you realize your dreams.

Becoming a smarter and sharper version of yourself isn't just about personal gain, it means levelling up for the greater good. When you improve yourself, you're not only setting yourself up for success but also making a positive impact on the world around you. It implies upgrading to a better version of yourself that can contribute more to society and humanity.

Keep striving to be the best version of yourself, because your growth isn't just for you, it's for everyone.

"You may not change the world, but your efforts can change someone's world."

So, as you close this book and embark on your own journey of growth and self-discovery, remember the lessons from *The Power of Ignored Skills*. Embrace the power of these skills, cultivate habits that serve your goals and never underestimate the impact of consistency. For it is in the daily rituals of our lives that we shape our destinies and create the future we desire.

All the best!

Keep shining and spreading positivity.

———•◆•———

ACKNOWLEDGEMENTS

First and foremost, I would like to thank God Almighty for giving me the ability and opportunity to write this book. Without His blessings, this achievement would not have been possible.

I am thankful to the people around me for their support, encouragement, inspiration and guidance.

The ideas, understanding and creativity we develop are the result of insights provided by many known and unknown people. Thus, I am thankful to each and everyone, who directly or indirectly helped me learn and shape my thought process.

I sincerely thank my brother Vinod Tripathi, who not only helped me in editing the book but also in enriching this book.

I am thankful to Banwari Lal Sharma, Harish Chandra, Saurabh Sharma and Smruti Jamdade for reading the manuscript and giving me valuable advice on how to make it interesting and useful.

I am thankful to all my teachers, professors and batchmates of Kendriya Vidyalaya, ATL School, AAIDU and IGTC.

Thanks to everyone in my publishing team at Notion Press Media.

I am thankful for all my family members' and relatives' love, affection and encouragement.

Most importantly, I am sincerely thankful to my beloved wife Suchita and my smart kids Riddhi and Trish who cooperated with, encouraged and supported me.

———•———

BIBLIOGRAPHY

Chapter 1: The Power of Observation

✦ Malcolm Gladwell, *Blink: The Power of Thinking without Thinking*, 2005

✦ Schultz, Howard; Yang, Dori Jones (1997), *Pour Your Heart Into It: How Starbucks Built a Company One Cup at a Time*, New York: Hyperion

✦ Kendra Cherry, "How Observational Learning Affects Behavior", Updated on September 06, 2019, https://www.verywellmind.com/what-is-observational-learning)

✦ "How observational learning affects behavior", https://ruachwords.org/how-observational-learning-affects-behavior/

✦ Prachi Juneja, "Curious Observation – First Step in Decision Making Process", https://www.managementstudyguide.com/curious-observation.htm

✦ James Clear, "Famous Biologist Louis Agassiz on the Usefulness of Learning Through Observation". https://jamesclear.com/louis-agassiz

✦ Dave Wedland, "Creativity Begins With Observation", 2019, https://www.forbes.com/sites/

forbesagencycouncil/2019/04/08/creativity-begins-with-observation/#4e838e622d40

Chapter 2: The Power of Connecting the Dots

✦ Pavan Kulkarni, "Amid Agrarian Crisis, India is Pressured By US to Reduce Farm Subsidies", 2008, https://www.newsclick.in/amid-agrarian-crisis-india-pressured-us-reduce-farm-subsidies

✦ Richa Kumar, "Putting Wheat in Its Place, Or Why the Green Revolution Wasn't Quite What It's Made Out to Be", 2016, https://thewire.in/agriculture/green-revolution-borlaug-food-security

✦ Bihar GK, "Freight Equalization Policy 1952 and Bihar", 2014, www.bihargk.com/freight-equalization-policy-1952-and-bihar/

✦ Joydeep Deb, "The Cobra Effect in Business Management", 2019, https://www.joydeepdeb.com/blog/cobra-effect-business-management.html

✦ Rob Dunn, "The Story of the Most Common Bird in the World", 2012, https://www.smithsonianmag.com/science-nature/the-story-of-the-most-common-bird-in-the-world-113046500/

✦ David DiSalvo, "How Alan Turing Helped Win WWII And Was Thanked With Criminal Prosecution For Being Gay", 2012, https://www.forbes.com/sites/daviddisalvo/2012/05/27/how-alan-turing-helped-win-wwii-and-was-thanked-with-criminal-prosecution-for-being-gay/#1044ab1b5cc3

✦ "Alan Turing", Biography.com, https://www.biography.com/scientist/alan-turing, 2014

✦ Marck Lorch, "Five chemistry inventions that enabled the modern world", 2015, https://theconversation.com/five-chemistry-inventions-that-enabled-the-modern-world-42452

Chapter 3: The Power of Communication

✦ "Verbal Communication Skills", https://www.skillsyouneed.com/ips/verbal-communication.html

✦ "Communication", https://www.toppr.com/guides/business-studies/directing/communication/

✦ Winston Churchill, "We shall fight on the beaches", Genius, https://genius.com/Winston-churchill-we-shall-fight-on-the-beaches-annotated?

✦ "The Fireside chats", 2010, https://www.history.com/topics/great-depression/fireside-chats

✦ National Park Service, "Roosevelt and Churchill: A Friendship That Saved The World," https://www.nps.gov/articles/fdrww2.htm

Chapter 4: The Power of Purpose

✦ Bard Leonard, "Why Is Life Purpose Important?", https://www.takingcharge.csh.umn.edu/why-life-purpose-important

✦ Jat Rana, "Career strategy: Don't sell sugar water", 2017, https://www.cnbc.com/2017/03/24/career-strategy-dont-sell-sugar-water.html

✦ Guusje Bendeler, "5 Reasons why purpose matters to employees", 2018, https://www.thinkparallax. com/Insight/5-reasons-why-purpose-matters-to-employees/

✦ Varun, "Dreams are very important", https:// www.killcure.com/2009/10/08/drea ms-are-very-important/

✦ Martin Luther King Jr, "I have a dream", https://www.americanrhetoric.com/speeches/ mlkihaveadream.htm

Chapter 6: The Power of Out-of-the-Box Thinking

✦ Mayo Oshin, "How to think outside the box and innovate new ideas", 2020, https://www.theladders. com/career-advice/how-to-think-outside-the-box-and-innovate-new-ideas

✦ George Friesen, "The $8 Million Replacement for a $20 Dollar Fan", 2013, workforcesolutions.stlcc. edu/2013/making-lean-stick-8-million-dollar-fan/

✦ Arushi Vats, "How an 'Ayurvedic' Vicks took over", 2016, https://www.livemint.com/Sundayapp/1rx2 BI7YhKE27460siRuyH/How-an-Ayurvedic-Vicks-took-over-India.html

Chapter 7: The Power of Perseverance

✦ Yogesh Sharma, "Talent is not enough, champions have attitude and the strength to fight – Perseverance", 2015, https://www.linkedin.com/pulse/talent-enough-champions-have-attitude-strength-fight-yogesh-sharma

✦ "Failures", https://howtosucceedwhenyouaredifferent.wordpress.com/2019/01/03/failures/

✦ Kevin Eberle, "10 Famous People Who Proved Perseverance Pays Off", 2015, https://www.business2community.com/leadership/10-famous-people-who-proved-perseverance-pays-off-01242413

✦ World Economic Forum, https://www.4martech.com/about-us/

Chapter 8: The Power of Deep Diving

✦ Farah Mohammad, "Why Are Diamonds More Expensive Than Water?", 2018, https://daily.jstor.org/diamonds-expensive-water/

✦ Carly Hallman, "A Timeline of Car History", https://www.titlemax.com/articles/a-timeline-of-car-history/

———•———

Scan QR code to access the
Penguin Random House India website